Praise for

ASHES IN THE OCEAN

Ashes in the Ocean is a beautifully written memoir which taps into what it means to live, love, and heal from grief and loss. It is a testament to the power of the human spirit.

—Mimi Guarneri, MD, FACC

President of the Academy of Integrative Health and Medicine

Ashes in the Ocean, the story of the loss of Sebastian Slovin's father from suicide, will resonate with many in our struggles to trust life and, no matter what, to stand in awe of the amazing world we are part of.

—James Hubbell

Artist

As a career psychotherapist I have worked with the aftermath of suicide too many times, and this book would have made my job much easier. Sebastian Slovin is courageously transparent in describing his process of healing from his father's suicide. As he so powerfully demonstrates, bottling up his feelings for years was destructive, and only by facing the facts head-on was he able to navigate these difficult waters. Not only is he an excellent storyteller but I would highly recommend his book to anyone who has experienced the suicide of someone close.

—José Luis Stevens, PhD

Author: Encounters with Power

Sebastian pens a brutally honest book that exhumes not only the ghosts of his father's ultimate choice but also his own relationship to suicide and mental health. Slovin considers the most complicated of human behaviorisms on a sectoral plane that transcends his own teenage angst and connects it with everyone who has ever dealt with a flawed legacy. He opens the vein of self-introspection by wondering why his hero left him with more than he could ever consume. But through this riveting memoir we see not only Slovin's transformation but perhaps a vehicle to understand—and ameliorate—those who are suffering and need the same attention as other serious, life-threatening pathologies.

—Scott Tinley, PhD
Faculty member at SDSU,
Author of Things to Be Survived and other life-transition-related books

Ashes in the Ocean is an eloquent story of a return to wholeness from a place of great darkness. Sebastian Slovin allows us to see not just the devastation of suicide, but the healing that is possible. At the end of his book I recalled a phrase from long ago. "Gentle is the way." Sebastian is a teacher for that way.

—Ronald Chapman
Author, A Killer's Grace and My Name Is Wonder

I experienced the same momentous event as the author. His descriptions are enlightening and compelling. I read *Ashes in the Ocean* in one sitting, simply because I could not put it down. I recommend it without reservation.

—Carol A. Edwards

Suicide is the leading cause of death in the United States. Globally, nearly 1 million people die by suicide each year, and these rates are expected to rise. Sebastian Slovin has written a courageous and moving novel about his firsthand experience of guilt, depression, and trauma associated with losing his father to suicide at a very young age. Slovin narrates his story across three continents as he confronts the stigma, silence, and complicated grief that surrounds his father's passing. Slovin uniquely reveals his own internal struggles and that of many surviving family members and friends who suffer from unspeakable guilt, shame, grief, depression, PTSD, and suicidal ideation on his journey to health.

Slovin's writing is clear, insightful, and accessible to many readers. To be honest, I could not put this book down once I began reading it. His work will inform, support, and inspire others who seek knowledge about suicide and survivorship. I *enthusiastically* recommend this book to anyone wishing to gain more insight into suicide, including trainees and professionals who provide education, support, and treatment to suicide survivors. Sebastian, thank you for writing this book.

—Ana Estrada, PhD
Associate Professor of Counseling, University of San Diego

Sebastian Slovin writes with the presence of his truth like the feet of the gods falling—thundering their way in from the heavens. I was moved into the depths of my heart within the first few pages, and stayed. If healing our suffering heals this world—these pages and Sebastian's words are medicine for us all.

—Janne Robinson
Poet

This book is about the lessons that a son receives from a father who has taken his own life. It is also about a man who comes of age and embraces his power by being curious, courageous, and compassionate. Through his fierce writing, Sebastian Slovin recounts his passionate quest to understand and learn from his father Vernon's suicide. He delivers insightful, timeless, and universal messages, which are at the core of the human experience.

—Stefano Olmeti, PhD
Global Leadership Coach

Brave, raw, honest, and, ultimately, hopeful. Among the many destructive legacies of his father's suicide was a deep-seated fear that the author himself would one day suffer the same fate. For years he tried to bury these demons deep inside and to follow societal convention by avoiding the subject altogether. When that didn't work, he decided to battle those demons by learning everything he could about his father and his father's decision to take his own life. It turned out his father's life, and death, had a great deal more to teach him than he could have ever imagined. Yes, this book is an inspirational guide for those of us who have lost a loved one to suicide. But, in fact, it is much more too. The author's journey exposes the dangers of a society that places too much emphasis on material wealth and status, while offering a practical example of how to avoid those destructive traps. And, for anyone who is afraid to face a difficult truth, whatever that truth might be, Slovin's compelling and engaging story will show you a path to a lighter and fuller future.

—John Cappetta
Business Leader and Philanthropist

There have been many books written about suicide and suicide prevention. *Ashes in the Ocean* is the best book I have read on how suicide affects the living victims and sheds light on how to deal with a personal tragedy. It helped me reconcile my own guilt about a childhood friend's suicide and the suicide of one of my soldiers years ago. Sebastian Slovin shares his powerful story about living in the shadow of his father's suicide and facing his own fears to choose a stronger path. Sebastian's journey began with an external search for all the "whys" of suicide, which led him to an internal discovery of light in the darkness of life. Filled with personal accounts, waves of vulnerability, and beautiful prose, Sebastian's book is extremely real, heart-wrenching, and wonderfully uplifting. Anyone wanting to understand the struggles of loss or wrestling with the aftermath and stigma of suicide should read *Ashes in the Ocean*.

—John M. Hinck
Retired Army Colonel and Apache Pilot
Author, Strength & Honor: 64 Stories of Leadership, Character, and Values

This book is a rare gift—beautifully and courageously written, heartbreaking, and deeply inspiring. It is a true story about the agony and isolation of growing up in the shadow of a father's suicide, and ultimately finding redemption and healing through the guidance and love of committed mentors and friends. Highly recommended not only for survivors of suicide, but for anyone interested in the human experience.

—Steven Alper, LCSW
Psychotherapist & Author, Mindfulness Meditation in Psychotherapy:
An Integrated Model for Clinicians

Ashes in the Ocean is a must-read. Sebastian brings light, awareness, and acceptance to the death and grieving process. Depression and then suicide, like addiction, are usually dark secrets that aren't discussed. Healing, light, acceptance, and then helping others are the keys to recovery. Reading his story and hearing how shame, isolation, anger, outbursts, distraction, and blame are all symptoms of unhealthy coping mechanisms which naturally occur in the recovery process will be helpful for everyone. Take some time and read this book.

—David M. Marlon, MS, MBA
Co-founder of Solutions Recovery

A book written with heart-wrenching courage and willingness to un-cover a personal tragedy and discover a gift of significant worthiness. Slovin shows tremendous insight into his own healing and journey. A must-read for anyone in the healing profession or who has firsthand experience with the loss of a loved one through suicide.

—Nancy Pollard, LCSW
Retired psychotherapist with 35 years of experience

While this book tells the story about a son coming to understand himself after his father's suicide, Slovin does so much more. In his open and honest account of his experience, he finds power in his voice and invites the reader to connect around courage, grief, compassion, shame, and facing fears and truths. Everyone will learn something about themselves from this book. Its power lies not only in the story but in the author's authentic search for understanding and acceptance.

—Lorri Sulpizio, PhD
Director of the Conscious Leadership Academy

Sebastian has always brought an infectious, positive approach to life, no matter what his circumstances. His ability to inspire others is not only sought after by many, but deeply appreciated by a diverse and vast audience. His community is far-reaching and the tools he shares on a daily basis provide the groundwork for a fulfilled life. Through this book, Sebastian shares his intimate experience with hardship and turns it into a story of love, compassion, and acceptance. His personal approach to heartbreaking loss and the ability to share the tools he learned come from a place of infinite gratitude. His book is not just a story of one, but a lesson for many to live and love like there is absolutely nothing standing in the way.

—Nora Tobin
Wellness Coach

Ashes in the Ocean provides immense value to the survivors of suicide. Those that live on, particularly children, are often haunted by the loss and the unanswered questions that plague their mind for years and, too often, the rest of their lives. Sebastian Slovin's authentic, open, and eloquent sharing of his story is the much-needed sounding board for those that live with the stigma of suicide. He brilliantly provides an engrossing pathway toward peace and healing that others can welcome and emulate. As someone who struggled through the unexpected loss of a parent in youth, I made connection to Slovin's grief, confusion, anger, and loneliness, but was strengthened by his honesty.

—Derek Abbey
West Region Director, The Travis Manion Foundation

ASHES
IN THE
OCEAN

A SON'S STORY OF LIVING THROUGH
&
LEARNING FROM HIS FATHER'S SUICIDE

SEBASTIAN SLOVIN

Nature Unplugged – Encinitas, California – 2018

Printed and bound in the United States of America
ISBN: 978-0-692-05119-1
Library of Congress Control Number: 2018901650

Cover photo by John Maher
www.johnmaherphoto.com

Design & layout by Isaac Mitchell
www.owlhousecreative.com

To my beautiful wife, Sonya Amira,
with love and gratitude.

The greatest binkers that ever was
and that ever will be.

LOST

Stand still. The trees ahead and the bushes beside you
Are not lost. Wherever you are is called Here,
And you must treat it as a powerful stranger,
Must ask permission to know it and be known.
The forest breathes. Listen. It answers,
I have made this place around you.
If you leave it, you may come back again, saying Here.
No two trees are the same to Raven.
No two branches are the same to Wren.
If what a tree or a bush does is lost on you,
You are surely lost. Stand still. The forest knows
Where you are. You must let it find you.

— **David Wagoner**

*From Traveling Light: Collected and New Poems.
Copyright 1999 by David Wagoner.
Used with permission of the University of Illinois Press.*

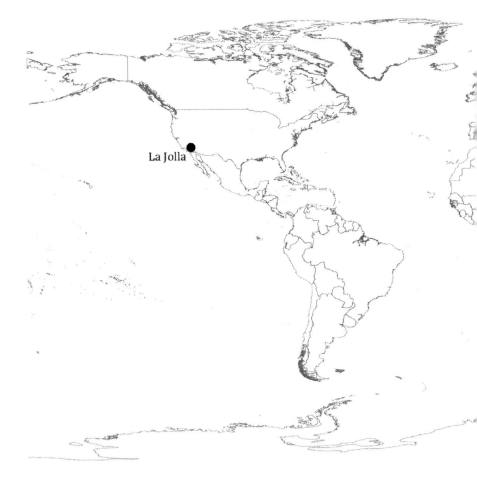

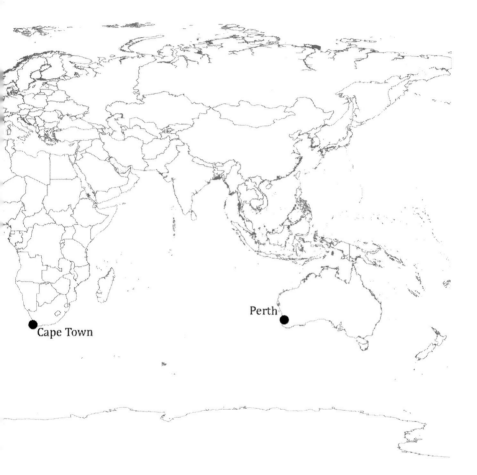

Perth

Cape Town

PREFACE

THIS IS THE STORY OF MY FATHER'S SUICIDE AND THE LIFE LESSONS THAT WERE REVEALED TO ME IN THE AFTERMATH. My intention in sharing this is to give voice and bring awareness to suicide and mental illness, which have for too long been buried in our society. This book is my stepping outside of the stigma of suicide. I wrote this, on a broad level, to help change the grim statistics and reduce the number of suicides. More specifically, I wrote this to help those who have lost a family member or friend to suicide. I've approached the subject not from the perspective of a neuroscientist, psychologist, social worker, or counselor, but from that of someone who has lived through the death of a loved one by suicide. I know what it's like to live in the shadow of such an event.

For many years, I felt trapped in that shadow. I even felt destined to follow in my father's fatal footsteps. I was fortunate to have had many great teachers and experiences along the way which have opened my eyes to the possibility of taking a different path. By sharing my story, I hope to shine light on the possibility of another way, a way out of the shadows. Beyond that, I want to show people that it is possible to move forward to a place of personal freedom and a lighter, fuller future. While this story is about suicide, it is also about the journey of becoming whole again and waking up to the beauty and wonder all around us.

TABLE OF CONTENTS

CHAPTER 1

THE COVE

We spend our life fishing,
only to realize it is not fish we are after.

—Henry David Thoreau

THE SWIMMERS JOCKEY FOR POSITION AS THEY TAKE THEIR MARK ON THE SAND. The main event of the La Jolla Rough Water Swim is about to get underway, the men's 35-and-under master's event. The tension and anticipation is palpable as the large crowd watches from the park above and surrounding lookout spots along the cliff. Each competitor, geared up in speedo, swim cap, and goggles, is poised and focused on the race ahead. Among these elite swimmers is Vernon Slovin, a 41-year-old native of South Africa. He often competed in younger age groups for more fierce competition. These were the types of moments Vernon lived for.

It's an unseasonably cold summer morning in La Jolla, California. The typically calm waters of the La Jolla Cove are churning with the strong wind out of the west. Whitecaps and waves texture the surface of the Pacific Ocean as far as the eye can see. Vernon gazes out over the ocean and the one-mile course. He is no stranger to these types of conditions; in fact, he feels at home in them. As he grew up swimming in the cold, rough waters around Cape Town, this was quite typical.

The announcement comes over the loudspeaker, "Swimmers, take your mark." The men assume their ready positions, with one leg in front of the other, knees bent, and torsos leaning forward, each swimmer with his own style and variation, ready to sprint toward the water. "Get set," the announcer calls out. *Bang!* At the sound of the gun, Vernon leaps ahead of the pack and sprints across the sand. He is the first to dive into the choppy water.

The crowd cheers from above as the swimmers move powerfully through the rough waters out toward their mark, the first of three large orange buoys making up the large triangle of the course. The spectators watch from the park and cliffs above the cove as the race begins to take shape. Vernon, in his blue cap, maintains the lead to the first buoy. Shortly after the second buoy, others in the group catch up to him. Over the next 20 minutes the swimmers battle it out, each trying to maintain a leading position. The balance of power and grace of each stroke propels the athletes toward the finish.

The cheers of the crowd grow louder as the group makes its way back toward the cove. There are five swimmers neck and neck, and as they make their way into the slightly calmer and protected waters of the cove, a young, powerful American separates from the pack and takes the lead. The American reaches the beach first, with Vernon just behind him and two other swimmers following, all within ten feet of each other. Everything now comes down to the sprint up the beach to the finish line. The American strides up the beach with the hope of victory within his reach. Just before he reaches the finish line, Vernon powers past the younger man and breaks the ribbon for the win.

The crowd cheers as the swimmers recover from the intensity of the race. With bent knees and hands on thighs, Vernon takes a handful of deep breaths and then smiles and waves to the crowd. Eight years in a row Vernon has won this event. The South African slowly makes his way up the stairs and embraces his beautiful wife, young son, and baby daughter who were watching from the park above.

I was the young towheaded son Vernon embraced after the race that day. My name is Sebastian and this is my story, the story of my relationship with my dad and the lessons he taught me. Many of my memories of Dad revolve around him winning one thing or another. He was a champion. He was a hero. He was *my* hero.

One of the earliest memories I have of my dad is when he showed me the secret of the conch shell. The large shell sat in the center of the rectangular glass coffee table in our living room. I knew the coffee table well, because I had nearly hit my head on it many times while roughhousing or playing ball in the house. It was a beautiful coffee table, although it did get in the way of my play space. Alongside the shell sat two large books, which I loved to look through. One had beautiful photographs of South Africa and the other of Australia.

"Listen closely," my dad said, as he held the shell up to my ear. I had examined the conch shell many times, but I'd never thought about listening to it. I looked up at him curiously. As the opening of the shell came closer to my ear, I could hear a faint but familiar sound. It sounded like it was coming from somewhere deep within the shell, a gentle hum like waves crashing far off in the distance. It was a beautiful sound.

"What is that?" I asked, full of wonder.

"That, my son, is the ocean."

"The ocean?" I said in disbelief. I took the shell and looked inside, hoping to find a glimpse of the source.

"The ocean was once this shell's home, and so it carries a part of the ocean with it," he told me with a smile. "Anytime you miss the ocean, you can just listen to a shell. That's what I do," he added.

I smiled back and continued to listen. *How could such a big thing like the ocean be in this little shell?* I thought to myself. I didn't quite understand it, but was fascinated nevertheless.

Listening to that shell became one of my favorite pastimes growing up. It was the next best thing to being at the beach, which was my absolute favorite place. At home, I would often lie on the floor next to the coffee table and hold the shell up to my ear, close my eyes, and listen. The soothing sound would take me away to the seashore.

When I look back on my childhood, it's difficult to remember much that didn't include the ocean. I was fortunate to have grown up in a beautiful little town in Southern California called La Jolla. La Jolla is an affluent coastal community to the north of downtown San Diego. I had a privileged upbringing with much to be thankful for. Of course, as a little tyke I didn't know that life could be any different.

There is something magical about La Jolla. The beach town is situated on the tip of a point of land, surrounded by either hills or the ocean. Its location gives it an intriguing sense of isolation and power. La Jolla feels like it's *the* place to be. Because of its location west of much of the rest of San Diego, there is a different quality of water and sand along its beautiful beaches. In many ways La Jolla has the feeling of an island, with clear waters and powerful surf. There is something in the air, an energy that is both welcoming and ominous at the same time.

Before I could walk, my days were spent crawling and exploring the La Jolla beaches and shoreline along with my mom and dad. I was fascinated by every aspect of that environment. The smells of the fresh, salt-laden air blowing in from the Pacific along with the usual scents of seaweed and sunscreen. The rhythmic sounds of the crashing waves and the call of the gulls were as familiar to me as my mother's voice.

Time took on a different quality along the ocean's shore. Although I spent countless hours at the beach during my youth, whenever I was in that environment I felt as if time ceased to exist. On one level, time was certainly passing; I grew older, the tides ebbed and flowed, and the weather patterns and seasons changed. But there was an aspect to the beach and ocean that seemed beyond time. As a child, I would often connect with this timeless quality. Whether I was looking out over the massive expanse of ocean or down at the tiny grains of sand running through my fingers, there was something about that environment that gave me the sense that I was part of something much bigger than myself.

I spent my early childhood years in a big house that was a short walk from a beach called Windansea, an incredibly scenic beach with rocky outcroppings of sandstone along the shoreline, which gives it a secluded feeling. Windansea is home to some great waves and is known for its surfing. The waves, which break over the underwater reef and then converge into a powerful shore-break, are great fun for experienced surfers, swimmers, and body-surfers, and quite dangerous for the novice beachgoer and small children. Some of my earliest memories are of getting blasted by forceful waves, tumbling and twirling around underwater, and eventually rolling up onto the sand.

My mom, Susan, would take me down to Windansea Beach nearly every day. It was an ideal upbringing, if I do say so myself. My dad, Vernon, would join us when he had a chance to get away from his busy work schedule. He'd play with me for a while and then disappear out in the ocean for his daily swim.

When we weren't at Windansea, we'd head over to La Jolla Cove for a change in scenery. "The Cove," as it's known, is a couple of miles north of Windansea, nestled along the protected side of the coast in La Jolla, which is less exposed to the wind and waves. The Cove was my dad's favorite beach in the area. As I got a little older, it became my favorite place too. Because it was sheltered from the powerful surf, the waters were typically clear and had a calm, pool-like feel.

One of my favorite things to do at the Cove was hold on to my dad's back as he'd swim out to sea. He would go much farther than I'd venture to go on my own. Sometimes he'd swim the butterfly stroke with me on his back (butterfly was his specialty). I'd try to time my breathing right—inhaling and exhaling, as we moved above and below the water's surface.

An amazing aspect of the Cove is that because of its sheltered waters, it's teeming with sea life. My dad would swim me out into the deeper waters, and along the way we would greet all sorts of marine life, including a variety of fish, my favorite being the bright orange Garibaldi. We'd also come across seals and sea lions, and the occasional moray eel. I was terrified of the idea of coming across many of these sea creatures alone, but when I was with my dad, it was different. With him I felt at home in the ocean. He treated these magical beings as if they were part of our family, and over time I learned to do the same.

The Cove became a second home to me. It seemed like all the locals knew my dad, whether from swimming or business, and by virtue of being his son, everyone knew me. Hanging out at the Cove was like a wonderland to me. When I wasn't swimming or snorkeling, there were tide pools and caves to explore, or I'd play games with my dad on the sand. Other times we'd just hang out in the grassy park overlooking the Cove near the small lifeguard station. This was a popular hangout spot for many of the local swimmers as well.

I loved playing cricket with my dad on the grass before he'd swim. He had given me a cricket bat from South Africa, and it was one of my favorite possessions; it had tacky black tape wrapped around the handle and beautifully finished wood for the bat. I would stand in front of a small tree, we pretended the trunk was the wicket, and my dad would bowl tennis balls to me while I defended the trunk and tried to blast away any balls that were on target. The locals cheered me on after a hit, as I'd run back and forth between the small tree and a makeshift base (a beach towel), the spot my dad bowled from.

It seemed like I was constantly in the water while growing up. While I enjoyed swimming, my favorite ocean activity was body-boarding, or boogie-boarding as it's also called. I loved the speed and rush of riding the waves on my boogie board. When I was just learning I'd stay close to shore, where it was shallow, and ride the waves after they had already crashed. I would ride a wave all the way up to the sand and then excitedly run back out and do it again. I could spend hours riding wave after wave, and often did just that.

On days when the waves weren't too big, my dad would take me farther out where the older kids and adults would surf. This was a big deal to me, because the water was deep out past the waves and I couldn't touch the bottom. The first time I went far out, I was scared, but with Dad by my side, I knew I was safe. He swam beside me as I kicked and paddled furiously on my boogie board, frightened that a big wave would crash on me and take me under. Once safely past the breakers, I'd watch in awe from my board as he'd dive underneath me and swim about like a seal. He could hold his breath for ages.

It was magical being out there with him.

"Keep watching," he said, treading water next to me as he pointed out toward the horizon.

"Watching for what?"

"When you're out here, it's important to always be paying attention to what the waves and water are doing. That way you'll learn how to read the waves and catch the ones you want."

"Oh, okay. But all the waves look the same to me. How do I know which one I want?"

"No two waves are exactly the same, Sebastian. Choosing the one you want will come from experience. Let's practice. You tell me which wave you want to take next."

"Okay," I said hesitantly. I wasn't used to these waves that hadn't broken yet.

I floated on my boogie board next to my dad and watched the water and horizon intently.

After a couple of minutes I could see the ocean level change as a series of bigger waves were lined up and heading our way.

"Paddle out!" Dad called to me, as he swam out toward the oncoming waves.

He stayed close as I paddled as hard as I could behind him. I could see there were four or five waves in a row.

"Let me know which one you want!" He called as I paddled over the first one.

As we made it over the second one, I called out, "This one!" The third wave of the set had my name on it.

My dad helped me turn around and again yelled, "Paddle!"

He swam beside me, and then just before the wave got to us, I felt his powerful push. I zoomed straight down the open face of the wave before it broke. It was the most awesome feeling in the world, like sliding down a steep liquid ramp. I held onto my board for dear life as the wave broke behind me. I nearly lost my grip as the white water splashed all around me. I maintained speed and made it out in front of the wave. I rode all the way onto the shore with a huge smile on my face.

I got off my board, stood up, and looked back at my dad. He was still way out past the waves with his arms raised, giving me two thumbs up. I smiled and gave him a thumbs-up back. I watched as he effortlessly swam into the next wave and body-surfed (without a board) all the way in to shore. Once back on the beach, he gave me a big high five, and then I quickly grabbed my board and yelled, "Let's do it again!"

When I was in the ocean with my dad, I felt invincible. However, without him it was quite a different story. In those early years I seldom went out past the breakers on my own. I tried a few times but either couldn't make it out past the broken waves or, once I was out there, I would get clobbered by a big one. When that happened, I'd head back into the shallow water as quickly as I could.

While I spent much of my youth in the ocean and was quite familiar with it, there was something about that environment that unnerved me. Sometimes my dad would go on long swims at the Cove by himself while I waited on the beach. I could track him in the beginning while he was relatively close, but then I'd lose sight of him. Just like that, he'd disappear. When he was gone for a long time, I would become convinced that something terrible had happened to him. He'd always return, though. He had a way with the ocean.

I, on the other hand, did not have that sort of comfort as a youngster, at least not when my dad wasn't with me. I feared the obvious ocean dangers, like getting eaten by a shark, swallowed by a whale, or worse, being dragged to the depths of the sea by some sort of giant squid or sea monster. More than the obvious dangers, I was afraid of going out into such vast and uncertain territory. While watching my dad swim, I was both scared for him and in awe of how he so often ventured into the unknown and survived.

The ocean was so immense, deep and mysterious. I often wondered whether I'd be able to swim like him someday.

My dad was a legend in our town of La Jolla. Born in Cape Town, South Africa, he grew up swimming in the rough waters off the coast of his hometown. He had an affluent and idyllic upbringing. He and his younger brother, Brian, were raised living part-time in a beautiful home overlooking the ocean in Sea Point, a wealthy coastal suburb of Cape Town, and part-time in a ranch house about 15 miles inland near Kenilworth, where they raised horses and had plenty of room to explore and play.

My dad's father, Samuel, a Lithuanian Jew, had come to South Africa with his family as a teenager. He arrived with nothing, and by the time he married my grandmother, Kitty, who was born in South Africa and was of English descent, he had become a prominent businessman in Cape Town.

My dad was a talented athlete and showed promise in cricket, rugby, and swimming. He excelled most in the water, and from an early age chose to focus on swimming. He began competing at the age of 10. Every morning his mom would take him to the local pool called the Long Street Baths to train. By the time he was 16, he began swimming for the Springboks, South Africa's national team, and traveled extensively, competing with the world's best. He held the South African butterfly record for 11 years.

In 1964, he was on the South African Olympic team headed for the Tokyo Olympics. But South Africa was banned from competition because of apartheid. Instead of going to Tokyo, the team toured Europe, and Vernon won the British 200-meter butterfly championship. During that time, an American coach saw him compete and offered him a swimming scholarship to Southern Methodist University (SMU), in Dallas, Texas. At the age of 18 he moved from Cape Town to Dallas to attend university and went on to be an All-American swimmer for the Mustangs.

At 6 feet tall and 190 pounds, Vernon had a stocky build, not the typical long, lean body of a swimmer. But what he lacked in natural build, he made up for with incredible willpower and determination. He was born with several large and conspicuous birthmarks, which added to the uniqueness of his physicality. His markings lacked any pigment and were stark white on his otherwise tan skin. The hair on his birthmarks was also white. He had large markings along his left calf, knee, and thigh, across his belly and chest, as well as a small mark on his forehead, which not only showed in his skin color but turned a patch of his otherwise curly dark brown hair to white. Both my younger sister and I were born with similar markings. My sister's marks were nearly identical to his. Mine were on the back of my left calf, across my chest and belly (although not as apparent as my dad's), and on the center of my forehead up to and just beyond my hairline.

After swimming for SMU for four years, Vernon went on to get an MBA from SMU. Upon finishing his studies, he made his way out west to San Diego, landing a job as a stockbroker. He made a new home for himself in La Jolla, which he chose in part because it was the most similar place to Cape Town that he could find in the United States. He was on the early side of a large wave of South Africans who eventually relocated to San Diego, and to La Jolla in particular. Within a short time he became well connected in La Jolla, and it wasn't long before he made a name for himself as a prominent businessman.

In addition to focusing on his career, Vernon continued to swim, training and competing at a high level. He entered the annual La Jolla Rough Water Swim—a one-mile swim in the ocean with 1,200 other competitors—in 1976, and won his age division. And he went on to win his age division each of the eight years he competed in it afterward. To make things more challenging, when he was in his forties he would enter the younger age bracket, 35 and under, and occasionally still win the entire race competing against collegiate swimmers. In 1980, he broke the world record in the 35- to 39-year-old age group for the 200 yards butterfly at a competition in Los Angeles, with a time of 2 minutes 5 seconds.

My dad was often described as an animal when it came to competition. He had the combination of ability and unbending willpower to push past mental and physical barriers in order to win. In our house the hallway walls and spare rooms were filled with shiny medals and trophies, along with numerous pictures of my dad in far-off places standing at the top of the podium. Even our garage was filled with boxes of his medals, trophies, ribbons, and other reminders of his prowess and winnings. It was clear to me from a very young age that winning was both expected and necessary for a successful and happy life.

My mother's story and upbringing were quite different. Susan grew up in Southern California in a suburb of Los Angeles called Whittier. She was the middle of three children, with an older brother named Daniel and a younger brother named Jeffrey. Her mother Doris was a schoolteacher, and her father Fred was a firefighter. She grew up in a typical suburban working-class family. She was a beautiful blonde with a sweet soul.

She attended the University of California at Santa Barbara, and after wrapping up her studies moved down to La Jolla. She found an incredible little cottage to rent just up the street from the Cove. She worked as a speech and language therapist in San Diego, and each day after work, it became her ritual to swim in the Cove. On the weekends she'd often hang out with her friends at Windansea Beach, which had more of a social scene. It was there on the sands of Windansea that my mom and dad met. He approached her and there was an immediate attraction. They hung out on the beach and swam together that day; the rest, they say, is history.

Shortly after they first met, Susan and Vernon had their first date. Susan had come down with a cold—nothing too serious, just a stuffy nose and sore throat. When she showed up at Vernon's door sounding a little congested, he asked in his thick South African accent, "You're not sick, are you?"

"It's just a little cold, nothing too bad," she replied.

After a long pause Vernon said, "I have the Rough Water Swim coming up in a couple of weeks. I can't take a chance on getting sick."

"Okay," Susan said, not knowing what this meant in terms of their date. "So, should we take a rain check then?"

"No, of course not. Don't be silly. We can just hang out here. I'll get you a chair and something to drink. You stay there on the porch and I'll stay in here on this side of the screen. That should do it," he said in a matter-of-fact tone.

After realizing he wasn't joking, Susan laughed and eventually obliged his strange request. The two went on to have one of their first dates and got to know each other with a screen between them.

Not long after they started dating, Vernon bought a beautiful home half a block away from Windansea Beach. It wasn't long until Susan moved in with him, and the two began building a life together. A few years later, on December 12, 1981, the two got married. It was the year that Princess Diana and Prince Charles got married, and inspired by the royal wedding, Vernon was set on having a similar experience. With over 300 people in attendance, the two got married at a Methodist church in La Jolla, and then drove a classic Mercedes convertible from the church to the beautiful and luxurious La Valencia Hotel, which overlooks La Jolla Cove.

The extravagant celebration went late into the night. The next morning, after a delightful brunch with the wedding party, the newlyweds headed straight for the airport to embark on their multi-destination honeymoon. Their first stop was Rio de Janeiro, where they stayed in a penthouse in the Rio Palace Hotel overlooking the iconic beaches of Ipanema and Copacabana. After an amazing stay in Brazil, they were off to explore Vernon's homeland of South Africa.

Their early years of marriage were full of travel, adventure, and prosperity. By the time I came into the world in 1984, my parents had settled into La Jolla quite nicely. They continued to travel, but were now putting down some roots. Vernon was doing great at work and they had finished remodeling the house. They were living the life they had dreamed of.

Four years later, my little sister came into this world. She was named Tanasa. The name is a variation of Tanasay, which is Swahili for the Ultimate One. Later my mom told me that while she was pregnant and thinking of a name for her baby girl, a few of my friends and I came up with the brilliant idea of calling her Fried Beans, which to this day I think would have been a fantastic name. Based on my name suggestion, it may seem like I wasn't too thrilled to start sharing the attention of my parents. However, I did come to appreciate my little sister, and a few years later considered her part of the family.

I grew up, as many boys do, idealizing my dad. He was like a superhero. Every morning he'd dress up in a fancy suit and go out and be successful as a stockbroker. Sometimes he'd take me to work with him. Even from a young age I could tell he possessed considerable power at work. Everyone seemed to have a great deal of respect for him. Then in the afternoon he'd change from being a businessman superhero to a swimming superhero. He'd hit the beach, throw on his speedo, and off he'd go, swimming far out to sea.

My dad was not only a great athlete but an intense competitor, and from a young age he groomed me to follow in his footsteps. My training began very early on. One morning, my dad dressed me up in sweatpants, sweatshirt, and shoes, and took me out to our pool. Without warning he lifted me up and tossed me into the deep end. This was done while my mom was away, of course. I remember struggling with the weight of the drenched clothes. I had only just learned to swim. My dad stood on the edge of the pool and watched, ready to help, but only if necessary. I struggled mightily to make it to the side of the pool. Gripping the side of the pool, I looked up at him in shock. He kneeled down and explained that most drownings happen when children fall into the water fully clothed and aren't used to it. "Plus," he said, "this sort of thing will make you stronger."

Soon I became comfortable swimming fully clothed. While I didn't appreciate those types of lessons until much later in life, one thing was clear: I wanted to do whatever I could to make him proud of me. He was my hero in every way, and I wanted to be just like him.

Every evening before starting our bedtime routine, my dad and I would go over to the bookshelf and sit in front of our Encyclopedia Britannica collection. Each night I got to ask any question that I wanted to.

I remember one night I asked my dad, "How many hairs are there on the human body?"

We looked it up in the encyclopedia, and he read me the answer, "There are hundreds of thousands of hairs on the human body."

"Wow!"

This was before I could read much, so I was never sure what answers came from the books and what came from my dad. Either way, I was always impressed and eager to learn more. After our nightly question-and-answer time, it was bedtime. My dad would tuck me in and read me a story from my favorite book, *Just So Stories*, by Rudyard Kipling. The book was filled with wild stories from far-off places explaining how different animals came to be how they are. My favorite was "The Elephant's Child," which tells the story of how elephants got their trunks. On a typical night, my dad would only get a few pages into the story before I was asking him other questions about elephants and Africa and what it was like growing up there. Reading time would turn into hearing stories of adventure and excitement from my dad's youth. I was fascinated by far-off places and the wild animals which lived there. Africa and Australia were my favorite to hear about.

In general, my early childhood was wonderful. My family was caring, supportive, and loving, and we had everything a family could wish for. We had a big house with lots of things. My dad had family and friends all over the place, spread between South Africa, the United States, and Australia, so we traveled extensively. From my perspective, life couldn't have been better; it was all just one big adventure. I would soon discover there was much more to the story than what I could see.

CHAPTER 2

THE SEARCH

No matter where you go, there you are.

—Attributed to Confucius

FROM MY PARENTS' PERSPECTIVE, THINGS WEREN'T QUITE AS CARE-FREE. While my dad had done very well financially for a time, shortly after I was born, he began to run into difficulties—the extent of which he tended to keep to himself. He had been working for a company named after its owner, J. David Dominelli. Mr. Dominelli turned out to be running a Ponzi scheme. While my dad initially made a great deal of money for himself and his clients, as the scheme collapsed, he lost much of his own wealth and that of others.

In the aftermath of it all, my dad found himself under a great deal of pressure to pay back those whose money he had invested; many of them were fellow South Africans living in San Diego. After this financial blow, my dad worked tirelessly to rebuild his business. As he struggled to rebuild his client base, he began to entertain the idea that perhaps San Diego was not the place to be.

He wanted to cut ties and start anew. Deep down, he wanted to replicate his upbringing in Cape Town. He sought the physical beauty and temperate climate of Cape Town without apartheid and the political and financial instability. He thought about all the places that might be a better fit and eventually decided on Australia. Reenergized at the prospect of starting anew in a far-off land, his next step was convincing my mom that it was time to move on.

My mom was skeptical at first, thinking of my sister and me and the impact immigrating would have on us. My mom's parents lived in Los Angeles and she struggled with the idea of being so far away from them. Eventually she came around, and we made plans to cut ties with America and head out across the Pacific on a new adventure.

On my sister's first birthday, February 11, 1989, my family immigrated to Australia. The immigration process was long and arduous, but as a five-year-old, it all just seemed like a big adventure to me. I spent most of the flight sitting next to my mom, who held my baby sister in a little swath. I sat with my face glued to the window, looking out at the ocean and watching the different types of clouds below. When I got tired, I curled up on the floor next to my parents' feet and napped.

While I was having the time of my life, my parents were certainly feeling the pressure. They were financially strapped and setting forth on a journey into the unknown with two crazy little kids in tow.

We arrived in Melbourne, where my dad had a few business connections. It didn't take him long to find work, and we settled into the groove of things relatively smoothly. Shortly after our arrival I enrolled in a school called Sandringham Prep, which was much more formal than anything I had experienced back home. I even had a little uniform to wear. Each morning I would put on my sharp navy blazer with a red emblem of the school and red trim along the lapel, along with a white shirt and khaki shorts. I had two different types of shoes, depending on the class. I had shiny black shoes for class and other school events, and then a pair of runners for playtime.

I drew a lot of attention, being the only American in my class. My funny accent no doubt created curiosity among my classmates. I transitioned into Australian life well and made new friends quickly. I think one of the reasons I connected with my new classmates so easily was that I loved sports. It didn't matter what type, I loved to run and move and play. Above all I loved to compete. I was fascinated with cricket and rugby, as these were sports I was familiar with but had only played with my dad. I remember playing rugby for the first time at Sandringham. I was so excited to finally get the ball that when I did, I forgot what to do next. I ran for a few seconds before getting clobbered by multiple classmates. These Aussies were not messing around!

From my perspective, this was just an extension of the awesomeness of my life in La Jolla. I enjoyed being in a new school and making new friends. I was fascinated with everything about Australia. The pictures I had seen in our coffee-table book were now alive and all around me.

The weather in Melbourne was very different from San Diego. Melbourne is located on the coast in the far south and eastern part of Australia, in the state of Victoria (not far from the island of Tasmania). While San Diego was typically warm and dry, Melbourne was cold and wet. I remember lying wide-awake at night listening to the powerful thunderstorms that rolled in from the south. I'd pull my covers up high and tight, providing as much comfort as possible while leaving just enough room for me to look out. My bedroom would light up bright white as I timidly glanced out my window. I'd stay up for hours watching the lightning and listening to the wind and rain hammer the house. I imagined that any moment the roof would be ripped off and I'd have to hang on for dear life.

While my world was rapidly expanding, my parents' experience was quite different. My dad was struggling. He had a job and things were okay; however, he was realizing that the potential to make money in Melbourne was just a fraction of what it was in the US. He wanted more; he wanted to be wealthy. My mom had her own set of challenges. Raising my sister and me while trying to keep my dad happy was no small feat.

After six months in Melbourne, my dad was convinced that we needed to move on. His new target was Perth, a relatively small but rapidly growing city across the country on the west coast. He had taken a business trip there and decided that Perth was the place to be. My dad had a cousin who lived in Perth as well as a handful of close South African friends. My mom was hesitant to pick up and move again, but my dad was relentless. He would go on and on about how perfect Perth was for us. He'd explain that it was just like San Diego, only far less crowded and even more beautiful. They didn't even have rush-hour traffic, he'd rejoice (he was always complaining about the traffic in Southern California). It was a safe and clean city, he'd say, a perfect place to raise a family.

My dad's search for the perfect life continued as we made the journey out west to Perth. When we arrived, we were graciously welcomed by our good family friends John David (or JD, as we called him), his wife Sara Kennedy, and their two boys John Jr. and Mark. The Kennedys kindly opened their house to us while we were getting settled. My father was right about Perth. It was a stunning city, much like Cape Town and San Diego in the sense that it was coastal with temperate weather and beautiful surroundings. It looked like Perth could be the winner.

I took to John David and Sara right away; their accents were different from other Aussies. Originally from South Africa, they sounded more like my dad. They were incredibly kind and treated us all like an extension of their family. Plus, I loved spending time with their sons Mark and John Jr., who at the time were 17 and 19 years old. I connected with the whole family, but spent most of my time with Mark. He was fun to be around, loved sports, and was willing to put up with me tagging along. The two of us would spend hours throwing the tennis ball around and playing soccer or basketball. The Proclaimers' song "500 Miles" had just come out, and some of my fondest memories are of cruising around in Mark's car listening to that timeless jam.

Vernon's cousin Tim lived just down the street from the Kennedys. Tim had three daughters, between age 16 and 20, and would often hang around with us. I didn't spend too much time with Tim, but would later come to know him quite well. To me,

Perth was awesome. I got to hang out with Mark and my cousins, and it was like being part of a big family, which I hadn't experienced before.

The Kennedys lived in a quiet suburb of Perth called Mount Pleasant. Their house was a short walk from the beautiful Canning River, which became a favorite destination for our family strolls. I hadn't lived by a river before and loved the way the water looked as it slowly flowed along, with big trees and grass on either side. There were also several parks and playgrounds not far from the house, right along the river. I loved being in Perth, because if my mom or dad couldn't take me to the park, I had Mark and John and my cousins down the road as options too. I spent as much time at the playgrounds as I could, swinging on the swings and climbing the monkey bars.

While I happily lived in my little bubble, tension continued to build between my mom and dad. Much of which I was unaware of. My dad was having difficulty finding work, and not long after being there, my mom sensed that he wanted to again be somewhere else. This was a pattern my mom knew all too well. The place he was recently raving about—with its beautiful weather, safe neighborhoods for the kids, lack of traffic and pollution—he was now beginning to complain about. *I'll never be able to make the kind of money here that I could in the States,* he'd say. Back to the good ole US of A he wanted to return.

My mom was becoming seriously concerned as my dad became more and more mentally scattered. He was swimming and exercising less and having trouble sleeping through the night. Wherever he went, it wasn't long before he'd find something wrong with that place. It was as if he had tunnel vision and became completely focused on the imperfections. Before moving to Australia, he would complain constantly about how crowded it was in San Diego and how horrendous the traffic was. This was one of a handful of reasons why he had wanted to move to Australia in the first place. Of course, once in Australia, the grass looked much greener back Stateside.

In August of 1989 my parents (mostly my dad) decided that Australia no longer fit our needs. We packed up our belongings and moved back to San Diego. My dad had his mind set on rebuilding his business. And, in San Diego, my mom could find a job in the education system that could bring in some stable income. Also, we'd be closer to my grandparents in Los Angeles.

As our plane touched down in Los Angeles, my mom looked over at my dad and saw an intense look of fear and regret. He was clammy and shaky, and when my mom asked him what was the matter, he shook his head and said nothing. She knew right then that he felt like it was a mistake to come back to the States. My sister and I of course were not aware of much of this at the time, but I was now beginning to sense that all was not well in the world.

After returning to the United States, it wasn't long before my dad's mental health deteriorated further. He had done a thorough job of burning his bridges on his way out of the country the year before, so getting back into the swing of things was difficult. Many of his prior business relationships had left him due to his work and ties with Dominelli, and he struggled to rebuild his client base.

He did what he knew best and what he had been trained to do as a competitive swimmer—he kept charging forward. He was set on reaching the finish line and realizing his dream of becoming rich and living in a big house on the beach in a place with little to no crime, traffic, pollution, or excessive crowds of people. He worked long hours to get things back on track. But his charging forward was to no avail.

My dad became so distraught over the reality of his situation that he sank into a serious depression. As his condition worsened over the next few months, he was eventually hospitalized. I remember visiting him in the psychiatric ward. I didn't fully understand what was going on at the time, but certainly knew that something wasn't right. I spent a lot of time in the waiting room and would often escape by playing with different games they had. My favorite games were those bead mazes, the ones with the different wires bent in strange and interesting ways and the little wooden beads of different shapes and colors. I'd push the different beads along a wild journey full of twists and turns. I was fascinated that no matter how windy the journey was, the beads always made it to the other side.

After I had played with the bead maze for a while, my mom would call me in to see my dad for a short time. He tried his hardest not to let us see him unwell and vulnerable, but I could tell something was wrong. He wasn't himself. I remember seeing him and the others there in the hospital and couldn't quite figure it out. There were no casts or wheelchairs; this wasn't like other hospitals I had seen. *What was wrong with them?* I wondered.

My dad spent six weeks in that hospital. It was an incredibly difficult time for my mom—trying to navigate visits to my dad while working full-time, along with taking care of my two-year-old sister and me, six years old. At this point my dad considered himself to be more of a burden on his friends and family than anything else. He didn't talk outright about suicide. He was, however, fixated on the idea of having some sort of an accident, and when my mom would visit him in the hospital, he'd often talk to her about this.

"I just need to figure out a way to have some sort of accident. That way you would get the life insurance and everything would work out," he'd explain to her in a matter-of-fact sort of way.

This sort of talk made my mom furious. "Do you think that's all you are to us?" she'd retort.

My dad was eventually released from the hospital. Back home my dad seemed different, like he was distant or hollow. The feeling around our house during this time was very dark and heavy.

One day while my mom was off at work, my dad did nothing but lie on the couch. All I wanted to do was play. I tried my very best to get him to play catch or go outside with me, but he barely responded. I remember looking into his eyes and it was like he wasn't really there; he was not quite asleep but not fully awake either. I couldn't figure out what was wrong with him. After a while I just let him be and went off and played on my own in my room. When it was close to dinner, I asked what we were going to have to eat. This shook him out of his funk for a bit, as he got up and went into the kitchen to prepare some food. He returned a few minutes later and lay back down on the couch and closed his eyes. After a while I fell asleep next to him. The next thing I remember is my mom coming in through the front door with my little sister, who had been at daycare all day. I looked around and saw smoke coming from the kitchen.

"Vernon!" my mom yelled. "What the hell is going on here?" She rushed into the kitchen, turned off the stove, and began fanning out the room with a towel. My dad didn't say anything; he just got up and walked into the bedroom.

One month after my dad was out of the hospital, he decided once and for all that he needed a change. Australia was the place to be. This time, however, my mom wasn't having it. She had found a steady job as a speech therapist at an elementary school in Carlsbad, a 30-minute drive north of La Jolla. This time she put her foot down and refused to go for the sake of my sister and me. She had just dragged us halfway across the globe, around Australia and back. We needed the steady income and stability for the kids, she would say, and that was that.

By this point we were in serious financial trouble. Through poor business decisions, my dad had not only lost much of his savings but had drained my mom's savings as well.

My dad would stay up all night pressuring my mom to go back to Australia with him. From my bedroom, I could hear them arguing late into the night, night after night.

My mom eventually told him, "If you're really serious about this, you can go on your own. As soon as you find a job and are certain about living there long-term, we will follow. Until then I just can't uproot these kids again."

I was midway through first grade, and she wanted me to have the chance to finish school before leaving again. The decision was at a standstill for several weeks, and then in the spring of 1990 my father made his decision to go back to Perth, Australia, by himself to look for work.

One morning my mom and dad had a particularly heated argument and things were very tense. My dad had been packing all morning. I was sitting by the front window when a cab pulled up and honked twice. My dad came over to say goodbye, and I looked into his watery eyes and saw tears rolling down his checks. He lifted me up, gave me a big hug, and made his way out the door toward the cab. I stayed and gloomily watched in silence from the open front door as he struggled with the weight of his two large suitcases. That was the first time I had ever seen him cry.

I can remember wondering when I was going to see him again. The cab driver got out of the car to open the trunk and help him with his luggage. "What do you have in here? Rocks?" the driver joked as he strained to lift the suitcases into the trunk. My dad gave him a meager but polite smile and looked back, wiped his eyes, and got in the cab.

The taxi had just started to pull away when it stopped suddenly. I could see my dad through the car window leaning forward in conversation with the driver. Just then my dad opened the door and got out. I could hear him apologizing to the driver. "I'm sorry. I'm sorry, I just can't do this." The cab driver, clearly frustrated, got out, opened the trunk, and my dad grabbed his large cases and slowly made his way back to the house. I was so happy to see him come back into the house that morning. I kept hearing him say over and over that he couldn't do it, that he wasn't ready to go.

His decision to stay with us was short-lived. Later that day he was back to weighing his options to stay or go. Two weeks later he finally made the decision to go back. This time, however, he arranged for my mom to take him to the airport while my sister and I were away staying with our friends, the Mahers, who lived a few blocks away. I don't remember saying goodbye to my dad before he left.

CHAPTER 3

THE CALL

~~~~~~

*What is life? It is the flash of a firefly in the night. It is
the breath of a buffalo in the wintertime. It is the little
shadow which runsacross the grass
and loses itself in the sunset.*

—Crowfoot

IT WAS MAY 10, 1990, AND THE PIERCING SOUND OF THE PHONE
RINGING BROKE THE SILENCE OF THE NIGHT. Jolted awake by the
sound, my mom rubbed her eyes and squinted at her clock to see
the time. It was 2 a.m. I hadn't been feeling well, and earlier that
night I had come to sleep in my mom's bed. My mom looked over
at me; unfazed by the sound, I continued to sleep deeply. Her
heart raced as the phone continued to ring.

She reached over to pick up the phone. "Hello," she said in a
sleepy yet concerned voice.

"Susan, it's me, Tim," came the voice on the other end. Tim,
my dad's cousin in Perth, sounded panicked. It was 9 a.m. on
Thursday morning in Perth at the time, and my dad had spent

some weeks with Tim and his family while he looked for work. My mom immediately sat upright in bed with a terrible feeling deep in her gut.

"Tim? What's going on? What's wrong?" she asked frantically.

With a shaky voice he replied, "I just came home and found Vernon dead. He's here on the floor of our living room. Susan, I'm so sorry. It was a suicide."

Completely frozen and shocked, my mom said nothing. She took the phone and left the room so she wouldn't wake me. As soon as she got into the hallway, all she wanted to do was scream. In disbelief she kept arguing with Tim, telling him, "No, that couldn't have happened," over and over. Tim went on to explain what he had observed.

"Everyone left the house early this morning. Sue (Tim's wife) and I were getting ready for our weekend camping trip. I just stopped by the house to pick up a few things before heading out. Vernon was supposed to be at a job interview this morning. When I pulled up to the driveway, the car wasn't there, but there were tire tracks around to the side yard.

"I turned off my car and quickly jumped out. I knew something was wrong as I followed the tire marks around the side of the house. I came around the corner and found our car in the side yard with the ignition still on. As I got closer to the car, I could see a hose running from the exhaust pipe into our living room. I followed the hose and my stomach dropped as I made my way to the door. There he was, dead on the floor with a trash bag over his head."

My mom didn't respond. She was in total shock.

"He left a note, Susan." Tim went on to read her the suicide note:

Dear Sue and Tim,

Sorry to spoil your guys' walk, but the pain is too great. I love my wife and my family so much, but events are beyond my control.

-Vernon

There in the hallway, my mom sank down to the floor and sobbed and sobbed. She was frustrated and sad beyond belief. As soon as she got off the phone with Tim, the thoughts and questions immediately started to pour in. *How could this have happened? Was there something I could have done to prevent it? I should have never let him go back to Australia on his own.*

Not knowing what else to do, my mom then called Richard and Derelynn Bonney, who were two of her closest friends. Richard and my dad went way back. He was a fellow South African and former SMU swim teammate. He and Derelynn probably knew our family dynamic better than anyone. They immediately offered to come over to be with her, but she declined. She spent the rest of the night trying to come to grips with what had happened.

The next day Derelynn and Richard did everything they could to lighten the load for my mom. They made many phone calls to pass along the news to friends and family. Our good friend Lisa Maher, who lived just down the street, came to take me to school. Another family friend, Sharon, took my sister to watch her for the day.

When Lisa came to the door that morning, my mom answered with bloodshot eyes, swollen from a sleepless night. Lisa told

Mom, "I can't say anything or I'll just burst into tears." After my sister and I left the house, the rest of the day was a blur for my mom. It was chaotic and filled with trying to process what had happened, along with making many calls to Australia and taking the necessary steps to take care of the administrative aspects of my father's death: Where will his body be taken? How do we arrange for his remains to be shipped over? How could we get the death certificate?

One of the calls my mom made was to a friend and therapist named David Heaney. David was also the pastor of the church we occasionally attended. She wanted some guidance on how and when to tell my sister and me what had happened. As a two-year-old, my sister was too young for any in-depth explanation, but David recommended telling me right away. I was six at the time. He advised telling me the truth and explaining that my dad had committed suicide.

That afternoon when I came home from school, my mom took me out into the backyard for the talk. We were lying on the grass as she explained what had happened. She told me that Dad was sick and in so much pain, and that he took his own life.

"What does that mean?" I asked.

"It means he has died and he's not coming back," she answered in a straightforward manner.

I didn't respond after that. I just lay there looking down, running my fingers through the blades of grass. I didn't cry. I didn't do much of anything. I didn't know what to do or how to respond. My whole body felt numb.

My mom was under immense financial pressure. With rent to pay and two children to feed, she was only able to take a few days off work. She didn't have time to process and grieve, as much of those days were spent arranging the memorial, getting the death certificate, and handling the details of my dad's death.

In the weeks and months that followed, my mom grew more and more concerned about me. My sister was handling it very well, according to my mom's friend who was a psychologist. She was having major tantrums, which was interpreted as her "getting it all out." I was doing the opposite. Where before I had been incredibly talkative and had an insatiable curiosity, asking questions about everything, now I wasn't saying much at all and had pretty much shut down.

One night I lay in my bed trying to fall asleep. I could hear my mom crying from her room next door. I hated to hear her cry. It was the worst sound in the world to me. I plugged my ears. I put my head under the pillow, but I couldn't stop hearing it. I was overwhelmed with sadness and confusion. My dad wasn't coming back, and now my mom was crying every night. I felt helpless and lost. It seemed in that moment that the safest course of action was not to feel.

I put up walls and tried to insulate myself from a world which now seemed dark and foreign to me. Instead of lashing out or getting upset, I began to withdraw. I spent more and more time alone. I would stay in my room as much as I could. I would lie down on the floor, close my eyes, and think about my dad and wish things would go back to the way they were.

There was a part of me that didn't completely believe that he was gone. *Maybe this is just a bad dream,* I thought. As the days and weeks passed, the hope that I'd wake up and things would be back to normal became dimmer and dimmer. It felt like the world had suddenly turned on me. I was living a nightmare.

CHAPTER 4

SPREADING THE ASHES

All things are one.

—Paulo Coelho

My dad's funeral service was held at the park overlooking the La Jolla Cove. It was a cold and gloomy day in May
when friends and family came together to pay their respects. I
recognized many of the people, and there were many more who
I didn't know. I watched as the large group gathered around. My
mom was dressed in black and was holding a bouquet of flowers.
She cried and cried as our family friend and pastor David led the
service. My godfather, Lydon, who was my dad's college roommate and SMU swim teammate, flew in from Chicago to deliver
the eulogy.

Here we were at the Cove on a cold gray day, my dad was gone,
and everyone was sad. None of it seemed real. After all, this was
the same place where I had so many wonderful memories of my
dad. The place where we would play catch and cricket, where we

37

would hang out before and after swimming. It was from this same place where I had so often watched my dad swim far out into the vast Pacific. Now everything was different.

At the end of the service I watched as people tossed roses over the cliff and into the ocean. At the time of the service my dad's remains hadn't yet arrived from Australia. Several weeks later when they arrived, my mom, sister, and I, along with our close friends Richard and Derelynn Bonney, returned to the Cove with his ashes.

We carefully made our way down to the rocks, to the water's edge. It was the same place where we had thrown the roses during his service. We found a small inlet of water which flowed in between the dark rocks. I watched as the water moved in and out as small waves pushed up against the rocky shore, occasionally splashing around our feet. I could hear the call of the gulls overhead and the occasional bark of sea lions that were perched on the rocky outcroppings just offshore. My mom proceeded to pour the ashes out of a tin container into the pool of water. The heavier ashes sank beneath the surface while others swirled and gathered on top. Slowly they all began to sink, merging with the water and sand. Small waves rolled in over the rocks and churned up the ashes until they were completely consumed by the ocean.

Like many things that happened during that time, I didn't fully comprehend what was going on. And although I didn't realize it, this event would change not only my relationship with the ocean, but my life in many ways.

CHAPTER 5

THE SWIM

In the middle of the road of my life I awoke in a dark wood where the true way was wholly lost.

—Dante

I WAS BACK ON THE BEACH AT THE COVE WITH MY DAD. IT WAS A BEAUTIFUL CLEAR DAY AND NO ONE ELSE WAS AROUND. I could feel the sand between my toes as I looked out over the huge expanse of water. We were getting ready to swim as we had done so many times before. He held my hand as we walked across the warm sand and into the clear water. It was warmer than I expected; so warm, in fact, that I could barely feel it.

I watched as my dad dove into the water and then swam out a few strokes. I put my goggles on and swam out to join him. I dipped my head under and looked through the crystal-clear water to see a few Garibaldi and other small fish swimming lazily below. I watched for a moment as the eel grass slowly swayed back and forth, moving with the gentle current. I looked ahead and saw my dad's strong legs kicking as he swam farther out. I lifted my head and swam as quickly as I could to catch up. He waited for me, and then I climbed on his back and he swam the butterfly stroke out beyond the protected cove and into the open ocean. I timed my breathing just right, holding my breath as we dipped under water, and then taking a big breath as we breached the surface and his arms swung forward. He swam farther and farther, until all of a sudden he dove deep. I panicked, knowing I wouldn't be able to hold my breath nearly as long as my dad. As we dove deeper, I was torn between letting go to swim to the surface and staying with him.

Just before running out of air, I had this strange feeling that I could breathe underwater. I decided to take a tiny little breath to try it out. I sipped slowly, like breathing in through a narrow straw, and to my amazement, I did it! Instead of water, cool air came in. Holding on to my dad's shoulders, I looked around in wonder at the beautiful deep shades of blue all around me. We explored the underwater world, swimming serenely past schools of fish and around long strands of kelp. It was the most peaceful and beautiful place.

Then, in an instant, my dad started swimming faster and faster. I tried as hard as I could to hold on, but could feel my fingers slipping until I lost him. I reached out as he swam off into the deep blue. He didn't look back. I yelled out for him, but nothing came out. I panicked and gasped for air, but couldn't breathe. I could feel myself losing consciousness, about to pass out, and suddenly everything went black. I bolted upright in my bed, gasping for air and clutching my throat. With a cold sweat and my heart pounding though my chest, I sat in bed, my eyes darting around the dark room, still searching for signs of my dad.

I rubbed my eyes and forehead, and tossed the covers aside to cool down. I swung my legs over the side of the bed, walked over to the window, and pulled aside the curtain. I stared out over the dark neighborhood and then looked up at the night sky. I used to love looking out into the sky at night, gazing up with wonder at the vastness of space and all the other planets and stars out there. Now, looking out into the darkness, there was no wonder. The shadowy world looked harsh, lonely, and unwelcoming.

The life I had come to know which was so full of joy, light, and freedom had been shattered. I felt completely overwhelmed. In the weeks and months following my dad's death I grew more and more closed off. To the best of my ability I blocked off, shut out, and pushed down the sadness, anger, and other emotions that were coming up. This was my plan for survival—I was not going to allow anything or anyone in to hurt me again.

Prior to my dad's death, my mom described me as being incredibly talkative and insatiably curious. I asked about how everything worked and where it all came from. *Why is the sky blue? Where do the clouds come from? How come the ocean water never runs out?* She later told me that after my dad died, my curiosity seemed to have vanished and I hardly spoke. I wouldn't talk about his death, and I shied away from talking about my dad altogether.

In many ways, his passing marked the end of my childhood. It felt like the freedom and innocence I once had was now gone. Death was something I hadn't had to deal with up until this point. Sure, I was aware that people didn't live forever, but it was very much in the periphery. I knew my grandpa on my dad's side had died before I was born and that my grandma passed away when I was very young. I had inquired about death, but it wasn't real to me then. Now it was very real. Death was front and center, and I thought about it constantly.

I would sit alone in my room and think about what it was like to die. *What did my dad feel when he died? What was he experiencing now? Was it just nothing? Was there a heaven or hell? Would I see him when I died?* It was all so mysterious. I developed a fascination with death, a sense of intimacy with it, but I wouldn't share that with anyone else. Facing death at a young age certainly played a role in my shift toward adulthood, as did my new responsibilities.

My life had suddenly gone from one filled with curiosity and adventure to one of responsibility. Without my dad around, I became acutely aware of how much pressure my mom was under. Now there were things that I needed to take care of, and I did whatever I could to help. This wasn't something I became aware of until much later, and it was part of a larger shift in our family dynamic: I was now the man of the family.

This shift in our family dynamic manifested in a number of ways. The new role I took on significantly altered my relationship with my mom and sister. I took it upon myself to help fill the void my father left, not aware of what I was giving up. I went from being a son, brother, and companion to a caretaker and parental figure. I began actively helping to manage the household and taking care of my little sister, who was two at the time. When my sister did something wrong, instead of telling my mom about it, I attempted to discipline her myself. This, of course, didn't bode well for our relationship. I was no longer a friend that she felt comfortable turning to if she had issues. I became another authority figure to her.

A similar dynamic occurred when she had problems and came to me for help. A few years later, she came to me crying because another girl at school was being mean to her. Instead of consoling her, I sternly told her that she couldn't act like this anymore and that she needed to be strong. Mom had too much going on to deal with her being a baby.

Similarly, when I got upset or something bad happened to me, I felt like I could no longer go to my mom for help. I was worried that I'd only add to her stress, and that was the last thing I wanted to do. While my sister could have been a great friend and resource for me to go to for help, I felt like I couldn't open up to her either.

When I was alone I spent much of my time dwelling on the past and on my dad's death. I wished and hoped and prayed that somehow I could undo things. I wondered if there was something different I could have done to make him want to keep on living. I wished that there would be some miracle and I'd just wake up from this mess.

When I wasn't thinking about the past, I would project into the future and imagine all the ways my life wasn't going to work out because my father wasn't going to be there to help guide and protect me. Sometimes I'd imagine an alternate future where my dad didn't die. I'd dream of scenarios where he would reappear as if nothing had ever happened. I would imagine him picking me up after school or him arriving home from work just before dinner. In this alternate world with my dad around, everything was perfect. We were one happy family.

Whether I was dwelling on the past and wishing things had gone differently or imagining either my perfect or hopeless future, I was left feeling scared and alone when I eventually came back to reality. To face my reality and to face my dad's death was the last thing I wanted to do. So, I did whatever I could do to escape and not deal with it. I kept to myself and pretended none of this was affecting me. On the outside, I still had the life of a kid growing up in Southern California. I had friends, did okay in school, played sports, and did the usual things that youngsters do. On the inside, however, things were different. My world now had a dark shadow over it.

CHAPTER 6

THE RACE

Winning isn't everything, it's the only thing.

—Red Saunders

SHORTLY AFTER MY FATHER DIED, I HAD AN INTENSE DESIRE TO COMPETE IN THE LA JOLLA ROUGH WATER SWIM. The race is held each September at the La Jolla Cove. The three-mile swim is one of America's premier rough water swims and has been a summertime tradition in San Diego since 1916. Since living in La Jolla, my dad had swum in the event eight years in a row and had won each time. For several years, he also held the record for fastest time.

My dad died in May of 1990, and the race was in September. I was six years old at the time, and to me it was an opportunity to honor my dad and follow in his footsteps. Or, perhaps this was a way to fill the void and emptiness I had been feeling. Regardless, I didn't just want to compete, I wanted to win. Prior to this point I had swum regularly with my dad both in pools and in the ocean but had not competed.

One morning at breakfast I told my mom I wanted to race in the Rough Water Swim just like dad did. She was fully supportive and told me, "If you want to swim in the race, you'll need to train and prepare like Dad did." I already had my sights set on the trophy and had overlooked the training part, but I figured that wouldn't be a bad idea.

A few weeks later I joined the La Jolla youth swim team. My friends John and Page Maher (whose parents Lisa and Michael were close friends of our family) were already on the team. John was a year older than I was and one of my best friends from school. His sister Page was my age and she was pretty cool too. I was excited to find that my entire new swim team had been training to compete in the junior course of the La Jolla Rough Water Swim. The timing was perfect.

From my first practice, I put a great deal of pressure on myself to be the best and to measure up. I was an intense competitor and showed a great deal of potential in the water. It didn't matter whether I was swimming, playing soccer, or kickball, I hated to lose. When I did, I'd spend hours sulking and thinking over what I could have done differently.

From a young age my dad had taught me the importance of winning. After he died, it only became more important. I understood what a successful athlete and competitor he had been, and I felt like I needed to be just like him. I became so obsessed with winning and measuring up that I was terrified of losing.

At the end of each week our swim team would have friendly competitions among our club. I won for my age group the first time I competed. After that, I was so worried about losing that right before the next race, I ran away and hid in the bushes. I hid until eventually my mom came to pick me up. She found me huddled in the bushes out in front of the La Jolla YMCA. Eventually, and only with a great deal of coercion, I agreed to come out. Running away and hiding became a common theme for me when the pressure was on.

Our swim team normally trained in the pool at the La Jolla YMCA. As we got closer to the Rough Water Swim, we started to practice at the Cove so we could get used to the course and the drastically different conditions in the ocean compared to the pool. I was swimming well during our training sessions, and my familiarity with the Cove was a big advantage. Even though I had trouble handling our weekly competition, I continued to set my sights on winning the big race. As the event grew closer, however, I became more and more nervous. In my mind, being the son of the legendary Vernon Slovin meant that I was expected to win; nothing else would do. Of course, this was all pressure I put on myself. My coach just wanted me to go out and swim my best, but the only thing I could think about was winning and the shame that would haunt me if I lost.

The night before the big race, I was consumed with anxiety. I thought about the race over and over and played everything out in my head. I thought about the possibility of losing and just couldn't bear it. I tossed and turned through the night and awoke the next morning in a cold sweat with my heart racing. It was early, and I could see by the faint light through the blinds that the sun was just starting to rise. I decided, there in my bed, that I wouldn't race, that I couldn't risk coming in second or worse.

A little while later I could hear my mom and sister moving around the house. I prepared for battle. Soon there was a knock on my door. It was my mom. She poked her head in. "Come on, Seb. It's time to get ready for the big race!" she said enthusiastically.

I pulled the covers over my head and yelled back, "I'm not going! I'm staying here!"

She didn't reply at first, but walked over to the side of my bed. She gently asked, "You're not going? But you've worked so hard for this. And you'll get to see all your friends. It will be fun."

"Leave me alone! I'm staying in bed. I'm not going. I can't go!" I shouted.

"Sebastian, there is nothing to worry about. This is an opportunity to have fun with your friends. It's not about winning; it's about doing your best and enjoying the event."

"No! You can go if you want, but I'm staying here!" I angrily replied.

Back and forth we went. She tried her very best to get me up and moving, but I wouldn't budge. Eventually this turned into a full-blown fight. I stalled in every way I knew how. I clung to the sheets as my mom tried to pull me out of bed. I refused to get dressed and wouldn't leave my room. I kept this up until I knew there was no chance of us making it to my race on time. Once I knew I wouldn't be competing, I finally gave in and gloomily got ready to go and watch the main event with my mom and sister.

By the time we arrived, the park and walkways overlooking the Cove were jam-packed with people. To my relief, the junior event, the race I was supposed to compete in, had already finished. Squeezing through the crowd, I looked down and saw my swimming teammates on the beach below. They had completed the race and were in their speedos with towels over their shoulders. I looked enviously at all of them smiling and laughing together, no doubt recounting the experiences of the race with each other. I was jealous that they had the courage to go out and compete. I felt the familiar ache of shame for not having shown up to compete. And at the same time, I felt smug and superior in a way; at least I hadn't lost. *I couldn't lose if I didn't compete, right?* I thought to myself.

I then looked around and realized that I was standing, among all the other spectators, right where we had held my dad's memorial service. I thought about my dad and what he would have thought of me being too scared to compete. The shame came on stronger this time. I felt like running away and hiding again.

"Sebastian! Come on!" My mom called to me as I was suddenly pulled out of my inner world. She and my sister were making their way over to get a better view of the main event, which was just about to take place. I gloomily followed with my head low and my eyes cast down. We had just found a place to sit with a good view when an announcement came over the loudspeaker.

"This race is dedicated to longtime competitor and champion Vernon Slovin, who passed away earlier this year. We will now take a moment of silence in his memory." I looked around at all the people bowing their heads. I was awed at how much everyone respected my dad. I felt a sense of pride as I bowed my head, closed my eyes, and turned inward. I could feel my heart pounding in my chest. The pride I felt was quickly evaporating and I was soon taken over by a deep and familiar feeling of shame and inadequacy. My father was so great; he was, especially in this moment, larger than life. How could I compete with that? Here I was at his favorite race at his favorite beach and I didn't even have the guts to race. After the moment of silence, there was a long and loud applause for my dad, but I didn't really hear it. I was too busy thinking about what a failure I was.

This feeling of shame, of not being good enough, became incredibly familiar to me in the years to come. I spent the remainder of the race trying to avoid running into my teammates or my coach. All I wanted to do was to run away, to leave, to go someplace no one could find me.

I spent a lot of time hiding after my dad died. My hiding took on many forms. There was a park on a hill a short walk from where we lived on Gravilla Street. Whenever I felt particularly lonely or sad, I would run up to the park and hide in the trees and bushes. I would find bushes with little hollowed-out spaces underneath where I could escape. I had a whole network of hiding spots that I would visit from time to time. I would crouch down low and wait until I felt ready to return. Often I didn't feel ready to go home, but I knew it would just add to my mom's worry and stress if I didn't.

If I couldn't get to the park, I would make forts out of couch cushions, pillows, sheets, and blankets. Although I was less isolated in my house fort than at the park, it was still a bit of an escape. When I was hiding, it felt like the worries and troubles of the world couldn't reach me. I wished that I could hide all the time.

Living in La Jolla was tough for my mom; the rent was high, and it was a long commute from her work as a speech therapist at an elementary school in the town of Carlsbad. When my dad died, he left us in bad financial shape. Shortly after he passed away, my mom was forced to file for bankruptcy. We couldn't afford to live in La Jolla any longer and my mom needed to be closer to her work. Wanting to keep my sister and me in the best public school system, my mom chose to move us to a town called Del Mar, which was about a 20-minute drive north from La Jolla.

Del Mar was out of our price range as well, although more afford-able than La Jolla, but my mom made it work somehow. This was just one of the many sacrifices she made to give my sister and me the very best opportunities possible. She worked long hours at her regular job and would see private clients in the evenings so we could get by.

La Jolla was my home. Not only did all my friends live there, but that's where most of my memories of my dad had been. I struggled with the move, but I knew how much my mom was sacrificing and didn't want to make things more difficult for her. At the same time, moving out of La Jolla also gave us, and my mom in particular, a fresh start. La Jolla was a small town, and the news of my dad's suicide trav-eled fast. There was also an added element of difficulty around this, because many of my dad's clients were wealthy residents of La Jolla, most of whom were fellow South Africans. Many were still angry with my dad because of the money he had lost for them prior to his suicide. With my dad no longer around, my mom now received the brunt of their anger and blame. She would often run into these former clients of my dad while out running errands or picking up groceries. It was like a breath of fresh air to move out of La Jolla.

Our home in Del Mar was within walking distance of my new school, which was great. I hated school, but loved playing sports before and after class and during any breaks we had. I didn't talk much in class, but it was there on the blacktop and on the field where I began to connect with some new friends.

While my transition into my new school was fairly smooth, I continued to avoid dealing with my emotions. I especially refrained from sharing anything about my dad with my teachers and classmates. I also did my best to steer clear of any activities or exchanges that might make me feel too much of anything. It didn't matter whether it was good or bad. I stayed away from any type of dramatic or emotionally evoking movies or games. When given the option, I refused to participate in such events.

When I was 9 years old, we visited our local county fair, the Del Mar Fair. We went with our family friends, the Bonneys, who had two boys, Cameron and Julian, who were a few years older than me. I always enjoyed spending time with the Bonney crew; they were like family to me. However, I didn't enjoy fairs and amusement parks. They were the absolute worst to me.

My experience of fairs and amusement parks was very similar to how I felt when, from the sidelines, I saw my swim teammates who had just competed in the Rough Water Swim. At the fair, I saw all sorts of different people with one thing in common. They were facing their fears, letting go, and stepping out of their comfort zones. People were going on crazy rides, playing games, and enjoying unusual foods and drinks.

I couldn't stand it. I felt like I was the only one there who was too scared to let go and enjoy it all, and that drove me crazy. Sure, I would do okay in the parts where we'd look at art or animals, but in the amusement park and roller-coaster portion of the fair, I felt completely alone.

While normally I avoided the fair, especially the rides, on this rare occasion I was talked into going on a roller coaster. Cameron and Julian were always trying to get me to go on one of those stupid rides. Typically, I would stand my ground and not budge. This time I let my guard down.

The ride looked pretty tame; we were in the kids' section of the fair, after all. *How bad could it be?* I thought to myself. The others could tell I was considering it, and that's when they pounced. All of a sudden, it was full-blown peer pressure. I eventually gave in and skeptically walked up the rickety steps toward the overly enthusiastic carnival worker. I handed him a couple of tickets to board the roller-coaster car, which from the platform suddenly looked a lot bigger than it had before.

I hesitantly got in one of the back seats of the roller-coaster car and pulled down the bar in front of me. The carnival man started the ride, and I gripped the bar tightly. All the other kids on the ride were excited and yelling, throwing their arms up into the air during every drop we took. My breath was shallow; my eyes were closed, and I held onto the bar for dear life for most of the ride. I hated the whole experience. After a few excruciating minutes, we came to a halt and relief set in, I was finally going to be allowed off this crazy thing. Or so I thought. Because it was toward the end of the night, the carnival man yelled out, "Since y'all are such a good group, how about another round?!" Everyone screamed out their approval. Everyone, that is, except me. I sheepishly raised my hand and asked if I could get off. Everyone else on the ride stopped and turned around. They all looked at me in disbelief. I didn't wait for the operator to agree; I lifted the seat bar and quickly scurried past my friends with my head low. I was out of there!

CHAPTER 7
THE SHADOW

We do not see things as they are. We see things as we are.

—The Talmud

As I moved into my teenage years and my understanding of the situation grew, I spent much of my time thinking of my dad and what happened to him. I remembered him as some sort of larger-than-life superhero. He had died before I had the chance to see him as a human. To me, my father became this all-powerful being, mainly because I refused to acknowledge that he had any flaws. Instead, I began to look at his suicide as an act of dominance over life, one where he was in control until the very end and life didn't have the chance to take him down.

He became a martyr to me, and in a way I began to worship him, or at least my memory of him and what he stood for. In my mind, this is what he stood for: Always be in control, always be the best; if things don't go your way, just keep charging forward, and if they still don't go your way, you can always check out. To me he represented control, power, and incredible will.

Every night before I went to bed I'd look at the picture of my dad that hung in my room. It was from his college swimming days at SMU. He was young, strong, and seemed confident and courageous. I'd look at his picture and think about everything he represented. And although I understood logically that things didn't turn out well for him in the end, I still found myself wanting and striving to be just like him.

While there was something about him and his suicide that I secretly admired, I was also constantly reminded of the consequences of his actions. It was very difficult for me to make sense of those opposing emotions and feelings. On the one hand, I admired him; on the other, I resented him deeply.

One of the most difficult aspects of my dad's death was watching what it did to my mom. She had so much on her plate just in providing for and taking care of my sister and me, let alone dealing with the emotional weight of my dad's suicide. She was often so stressed and exhausted that it seemed she would break down at any moment. Only, she didn't. Like the Energizer Bunny, she kept going and going, meeting the demands that life placed on her.

My sister and I were incredibly fortunate that my mom had the courage and strength that she did. The resilience she showed during that time was amazing. However, it did come at a price. Because of the financial pressure, my mom didn't have the luxury to take time off to grieve, so she did what she had to do to survive. Anything that wasn't crucial for survival was pushed aside. In this case, it meant her emotions and feelings around the suicide. She simply didn't have the time to process what had happened.

While my survival response to my dad's death was to isolate and hide, my mom's was to work her ass off and do whatever was necessary to make sure my sister and I got through this. She not only worked her regular job as a speech and language therapist, but also took on private clients, whom she worked with after her day job to make ends meet.

At work, in the months following my dad's death, my mom would often break down and cry in her classroom when she was alone, in between working with her students. She would often drive off campus during her lunch hour, find an empty parking lot somewhere, and cry the tears that needed to be wept. She even bought special waterproof makeup so that her co-workers and students wouldn't know she had been crying.

My mom was so focused on survival that when she wasn't working or taking care of something critically important, she was left completely drained. It was as if the spark and fun had been taken out of life. Most of my memories of her during the years after my dad's death are of her working, taking care of some practical aspect of life, like cooking, cleaning, or paying bills, or of her resting. Resting either meant completely zonked out asleep (with the TV on), or reading (with the TV on), or just plain watching TV. When she was home, the television was constantly on.

I would often find cups of tea around the house in various places. The cup would be full of cold, overbrewed tea with the bloated tea bag floating on the surface. My mom did all the things—worked, cleaned, cooked, made the tea—but didn't have the time, or wasn't able to take the time, to enjoy the tea she had prepared. While I was isolating myself, she was distracting herself.

While I thought about my dad's suicide a great deal, growing up we very rarely spoke about the nature of his death. Sure, we alluded to it at times, tiptoeing around the proverbial elephant in the room, but we never spoke about it directly. For many years, we never even said the word "suicide." Suicide was like our version of Lord Voldemort or *He who must not be named* in the world of Harry Potter. The word was something that loomed over us. It held great unspoken meaning and represented a whole world of guilt and shame by association. And, while we avoided using the word "suicide" or talking about it, it certainly had a deep impact on my mother, sister, and me. For much of my life, the stigma around suicide was lurking just beneath the surface. I was aware of it, but couldn't see it clearly.

There were so many unanswered questions with my dad's suicide. And because of the stigma, these questions were often cloaked in guilt and shame. Why did this happen to *my* dad? Was there something about *me* that contributed to his death? Is there something wrong with *me,* with *my* family? Some of the stigma I felt around suicide certainly came from my own doing and think-ing. And at the same time, a good portion of it came from the views of society and those around me.

We didn't talk about suicide at home, and one thing I learned early on was not to talk about it outside the home either. As I got older and my curiosity grew stronger, there were times when I did share with others what had happened to my dad. During those infrequent times that I talked about it, the responses I got certainly did not encourage me to share more.

I remember getting a physical exam when I was 13, and the doctor asked me about my family health history. She asked about my mom's side of the family, and that was fairly straightforward.

"And what about your father's side?" she asked.

"Well, my dad died when I was young, and I don't know much about my grandparents. They died before I was born," I replied nervously.

"Okay, and how did your father die?" she inquired.

There was a long pause.

"It was suicide," I said quietly, looking down and avoiding eye contact.

"Suicide," she said, sounding worried and surprised. I looked up at her for a moment and then turned my eyes down again.

Now taking a more serious tone, she went on. "Listen to me. You must be very careful with this, Sebastian. Studies show that you are much more likely to be depressed or suicidal when it's in your family like this. You see, it's in your genes."

I immediately regretted sharing about my dad. After doing so, I felt like she was looking at me differently, speaking to me differently, treating me differently, like there was something wrong with me.

She then went on to ask me a series of other questions regarding my mental health. "Have you ever been depressed? Have you ever thought about committing suicide yourself?" I denied having even the slightest of issues with my mental health. I wanted the conversation, the appointment, all of it, to be over.

At the time, all I felt was judgment—judgment that there was something wrong with me, and not just with me but with my family, my bloodline. I felt like I had been marked. Her response only reconfirmed the thoughts of shame and judgment that I had carried with me since my dad's death. Her response left a deep and lasting imprint in my mind; that if I opened up about suicide, judgment and shame would follow. This only reinforced my belief that this aspect of my life and of my family history was to be buried and kept hidden beneath the surface.

Growing up having lost a member of my family to suicide, I quickly became aware of our societal stigma around it. While there were exceptions, people who responded with heartfelt care and compassion, the majority of the time when I spoke about my dad's suicide or when someone found out about it from a different source, the stigma and shame around it was palpable.

When I was 16, my mom and I had one of only a few conversations I can remember about Dad's suicide. It was then that I gained further insight into her experience of losing her husband to suicide. During our talk, she told me about a series of conversations she had with my Uncle Brian, my dad's brother, shortly after my dad's death. I knew of him, but had virtually no relationship with him. He, like my dad, had immigrated to the United States from South Africa. He now lived in Texas with his family and kept quite separate from us. I had the sense that he wasn't very supportive of my mom after my dad's death, but didn't know much else.

My mom explained to me that when she told Brian that Vernon had died and that it was suicide, he immediately blamed her. She tried to explain the circumstances (Brian and my dad hadn't spoken much in the months prior to his death), the financial issues, and his struggle with depression, and no matter what my mom said, his response was, "But, Susan, you were his wife. You could have done something. You should have done something to stop him!" At the time, I was outraged that Brian could have said those things to my mom. He had no idea what was going on with my dad at the time, and here he was blaming my mom for my dad's actions.

It was these types of conversations that fueled the stigma within the family around suicide. My mom learned from that conversation and others like it that it wasn't safe to open up about Vernon's suicide, even with family. If she did, she would risk being judged, blamed, and shamed. To me, the most painful thing about hearing this from my mom was not the accusation from my Uncle Brian, but that I could see there was a part of her that believed Brian was right. I could see it in her face, I could hear it in her voice. Maybe she wasn't fully conscious of it, but it was there. And the truth is that I felt the same way; even if it wasn't a logical thought, it was there beneath the surface. On some level, I believed it was our fault as a family or my fault as his son. Many of these beliefs were the effects of the stigma around suicide that we experienced; they were the breeding ground of shame and guilt in me and my family.

During family gatherings, the subject of suicide was never broached. From a young age, I noticed that if the subject of my dad came up or his name was mentioned, the topic would quickly be changed. It was an unspoken rule throughout my extended family on my mom's side. While they were kind and caring, there were many topics and events that simply weren't spoken of. The way we as a family dealt with trauma and loss was to avoid it. For the most part, anything that was emotionally charged was off the table. All this was unspoken, of course. While this kept the peace in the family and kept things safe and comfortable, it taught me that suicide was not okay to talk about. In fact, there was nothing okay about it.

Twenty years later this feeling of shame still lingers in our family like a chronic disease. Just recently I was out at breakfast with my mom. We were catching up as we waited for our food. I asked her how her week had been going, and she shared with me that she recently got together with her good friend Kathleen.

"How's Kathleen doing?" I asked.

"She's been doing well. She's retired now and has been traveling a lot," she replied. And then her tone changed.

"You remember Kathleen's friend Zora?" she said in a hushed voice, leaning in.

I nodded yes.

She continued, "Well, I just heard from Kathleen that Zora's husband recently died of circumstances similar to your dad's."

Although I got the gist of what she meant, I was struck by how, years later, and after many conversations on the subject of suicide, she chose to say "circumstances similar to your dad's" as opposed to suicide.

So I asked, "What do you mean?"

She leaned in and in a shaky voice said, "He committed suicide."

"Why didn't you just say it?" I asked.

"Because I was ashamed," she replied.

I didn't know what to say in response to that. I just looked at her. She sat staring down at her plate with her shoulders rounded forward and her hands in her lap. Now in her midsixties, a few strands of her graying blonde hair had fallen in front of her face. I felt for her; it was one of those moments where I could see the weight of years of stigma and shame she was carrying.

This type of taboo and shame around suicide gave it a great deal of power when I was growing up. Feeling like I couldn't talk about my dad created a large barrier between the rest of my family and me. I felt this way not only with my family, but in most relationships as well. I constantly felt like I was hiding something, like I had to keep my guard up. This dynamic led to me feeling isolated, and it fueled my sense that there was something terribly wrong with me, something looming inside that would one day emerge and rear its ugly head.

I imagine that I wasn't alone in feeling isolated and that my mom and sister felt similarly. Looking back, it's painful for me to think of the amount of emotional turmoil that the three of us were carrying and that we didn't know how to be there for each other. I think one of the main barriers to us doing a better job of supporting each other had to do with fear of and inability to talk about my dad's suicide.

I was either scared or angry for much of my youth. I spent so much energy protecting myself and not letting others in that I was often exhausted and run-down. Every so often, I would crack in public and either break down crying or have an outburst of anger for no apparent reason. I remember one time early on in high school I was hanging out with a group of friends, some I knew well and some I was just getting to know. We were messing around, exploring a half-built construction site on the edge of the suburbs not far from where I lived. We were out throwing rocks and climbing fences like normal, and one of my friends was talking about a camping trip he was about to take with his father. I was walking along and listening, not saying much as usual, and I just started to cry. Thoughts came up about my father and why he wasn't around, and I completely broke down. I sobbed and sobbed and couldn't stop. No one knew what was going on with me, and some of the kids started to tease me. At the time, I didn't even know what was going on with me. There was nothing I could do to stop the tears from coming.

I had breakdowns like this throughout middle school and high school. Sometimes I would just start crying for seemingly no reason at all. Other times I would explode in anger. I was suspended in middle school for hitting a classmate in the locker room after PE. He made a comment that upset me, and I lashed out. I had similar instances of anger on the soccer field. I would get into fights with people on my own team, sometimes for little more than someone looking at me the wrong way. I didn't have much awareness around these episodes. They seemed sporadic and random, and I couldn't figure them out. I interpreted it as more evidence that deep down something was wrong with me, and from time to time the monster crept out of the shadows. In hindsight, I see those outbursts as evidence that my way of surviving and dealing with my dad's death—running away from and suppressing my feelings—was not sustainable. I was starting to crack.

CHAPTER 8

THE OCEAN

*Nothing in the world is as soft and yielding as water.
Yet for dissolving the hard and inflexible, nothing can
surpass it. The soft overcomes the hard; the gentle
overcomes the rigid. Everyone knows this is true,
but few can put it into practice.*

—Lao Tzu

ALTHOUGH MUCH OF MY CHILDHOOD WAS DARK AFTER MY FATHER DIED, WHEN I WAS AT THE BEACH OR IN THE OCEAN, THINGS WERE DIFFERENT. There, all the vibrancy of life was restored. Most of the memories I have of my dad have something to do with the beach or the ocean. While the ocean had always been special to me, after he died, it became much more than that; it became my refuge. Whenever I felt sad, lost, or lonely, if I could just get myself down to the beach, my perspective would change. Once I was there, I knew I'd be okay.

Growing up, my dad had taught me to love and respect the ocean as if it was part of our family—an idea I resonated with, but didn't fully embrace. I would often think back to when we spread my dad's ashes in the ocean. From that moment on, I saw my father and the ocean as one. The idea of loving the ocean as if it were family took on a whole new meaning. It was no longer just a concept to me; it was real. At the beach or in the ocean, I knew my dad was right there with me. I saw him in the sand, the water, the seaweed, in the dolphins, fish, and seals swimming by; he was there in every aspect of that wild world.

Going to the beach then became much more than a routine thing for me; it became a sacred experience. When I would visit the ocean, everything seemed to slow down. I was present with every step and every breath I took. All my senses became filled with my surroundings. My time at the beach and in the water gave me the strength and determination to keep going back on dry land, making it through the loneliness and pain of my day-to-day existence. I'd return from the ocean renewed and recharged. It was my power source; it was my home.

When I spent time in the ocean, I was so intensely focused and absorbed in that particular moment that it did not allow for any worries or problems to touch me. It was the only place where I could be fully present and at peace. Anything that wasn't with me right at that moment seemed to fade away; even my sense of time disappeared. The ocean was most definitely an escape for me, an escape that probably saved my sanity. But more than an escape, those experiences in the ocean were my first glimpses into the possibility of being completely present in the here and now. And for a long time, the ocean remained my only access point to the present moment.

In many ways, it felt like I was living two lives; I felt free and full of wonder in the ocean and isolated and numb on land. I became obsessed with spending time in the ocean. I enjoyed all sorts of activities at the beach and in the water, whether it was playing in the sand, swimming, bodysurfing, or surfing. My favorite ocean activity was bodyboarding. After my dad died, bodyboarding was the closest thing I had to being with him again. I could be out there for hours and not get bored.

When I was in 7th grade, I joined the school surf and body-board team. This was an opportunity to compete against other middle schools in the region. I struggled in the contests that year, especially in the beginning, rarely moving past the first round. My experience in competition with bodyboarding was markedly different from my short-lived competitive swimming career. With bodyboarding I didn't feel the same pressure that I felt with swim-ming. Bodyboarding was something that I loved, and it felt much more like play than anything else. My struggles in competition weren't because of the pressure I put on myself, but because I was new to competition in the sport. Because I was passionate about it, I stuck with it, and out of all my friends and teammates, I probably spent the most time in the water. For that reason, along with my competitiveness, I progressed quickly. The ocean was like a second home to me, and my passion was turning into an obses-sion. In the summer between 7th and 8th grade, I spent a ridic-ulous amount of time in the ocean, and loved every minute of it.

By 8th grade my bodyboarding had improved dramatically. I was now making it to the finals in most competitions and ended up winning a handful that year. At the end of the year

I was invited to compete in the California State Surfing and Bodyboarding Championships up north in Huntington Beach. The waves were mediocre, but I was bodyboarding with confidence and felt in the zone. I won each heat that day and ended up winning the entire competition.

Winning the state championship helped take my bodyboarding to the next level. From there I landed a few sponsors, and throughout high school bodyboarding was my number one priority. I attribute my survival to my connection with nature through riding the waves. I continued to grow and improve and would soon be competing at a professional level.

I found solace in and around the ocean. With my bodyboarding, I had an activity to focus my attention. It was something that gave me an outlet for the anger and sadness that I had buried beneath the surface. It gave me a way to be creative and competitive while feeling connected to something larger than myself. While my time in the ocean was critical for my well-being and survival, back on land I continued to struggle, keeping everything bottled up inside.

CHAPTER 9

STEPPING INTO THE PAST

*Courage starts with showing up and
letting ourselves be seen.*

—Brené Brown

DURING THE SUMMER BETWEEN MY FIRST AND SECOND YEAR OF HIGH
SCHOOL I GOT A CALL FROM MY GODFATHER, LYDON. After catching up
for a few minutes, Lydon said, "Seb, I'm calling because I'm planning
a trip to SMU for homecoming weekend this November." (Southern
Methodist University in Dallas, Texas, was my father and Lydon's alma
mater.) "If you're interested, I'd like for you to join me," he offered.

"That would be great!" I replied, without hesitation.

"Wonderful. I think you'd enjoy seeing where your dad and
I went to school. Plus, it's athletic alumni weekend, so a lot of
our old swim teammates will be there," he continued. "Okay, I've
got to run, but I'll follow up with you and your mom regarding
details. I'll arrange the flight and everything so you don't have to
worry about that."

"Okay, awesome. Thank you, Lydon," I said, and hung up the phone.

A few months later I was on a flight headed for Dallas. I was 16 at the time and didn't know what to expect. I was excited about the trip. I always enjoyed spending time with Lydon, and I was looking forward to seeing where he and my dad went to school. At the same time, I was nervous about what I might have to face.

Lydon was there to meet me at the airport when I arrived. He had flown in from Chicago a few hours earlier. Lydon had been my dad's roommate in college and one of his closest friends from then on. He and his wife Linda lived in Chicago and had two children who were a few years older than my sister and me. We didn't have the opportunity to see them all that often, but whenever we did, it was a big deal. They were like family to us, and Lydon was in many ways like a father to me. He was a clean-cut, distinguished-looking man. He was remarkably fit and energetic for someone in his midfifties. He came across as confident, but was also very approachable and humble. He had known me since the day I was born and was someone who had always been there for me. At the same time, he never pushed me to talk about anything if I wasn't up for it.

We arrived in the afternoon and checked into our hotel, not far from the SMU campus just north of downtown Dallas. It was homecoming as well as athletic alumni week, and the hotel was filled with folks who had in years past played one sport or another for SMU.

After grabbing a bite to eat at an amazing little deli, we drove onto campus, where Lydon was going to give me a tour of all the old spots he and my father used to frequent. I was blown away by how beautiful the campus was, with the Southern-style brick architecture and all the huge trees. The feel was completely different from that of Southern California. Walking across the grounds that my father once walked was an amazing experience. Lydon shared with me all sorts of stories about the swim team and the mischief they got up to.

Walking up a wide set of stairs, Lydon pointed to a large white pillar nearby. "This was one of our favorite spots to people-watch. Your dad and I would meet here after class. We'd hang out and practice chatting up the girls who walked by. Vernon was always very popular with the ladies. I think it was his accent," he said with a smile. We took a moment on the staircase and I imagined what life was like for the two of them here back in the late '60s and early '70s.

After exploring the campus for a while, Lydon checked his watch and said, "Let's head over to the pool. Some of the guys should be there by now. Come on, this way," he said, pointing to a large auditorium in the distance. We made our way across a beautifully manicured lawn and arrived at the entrance to the building that housed the pool Lydon and Vernon had trained and competed in. The spacious auditorium was mostly empty when we walked in. It was warm and humid inside, with a strong smell of chlorine, typical of indoor pools. There were a few people swimming laps and a small gathering of people on the far side of the pool.

Lydon recognized the group and said, "Some of these guys swam with your father and me. Come on, there are a few people I'd like to introduce you to."

As we walked over, I watched the swimmers going back and forth. I thought back to the days when my dad had been here. This pool and auditorium felt like a holy place to me.

Lydon introduced me to the group, who were all former SMU swimmers. Some had known my dad well and others had only heard of him. I was told repeatedly how much of a legend my dad was by those he swam with. They shared stories of how he would train longer and harder than anyone else. Some of them knew my father had passed away and expressed their condolences, while others asked me how he was doing. For those who didn't know how he had passed, at first I felt pulled to lie and tell them he had been in a car accident or something like that. I'm not sure if it had to do with the location or being with Lydon, but this was one of the first times when I consciously decided it was important for me to stand and be truthful about my dad's death. I gathered my strength and told his old swim teammates that he had died of suicide. There was something within me that knew I needed to face my dad's death. And being honest about it with others was a step in that direction.

As I shared about my dad's suicide with one of his teammates, a few others overheard and stepped in, making a bigger circle. Lydon had also overheard what I was saying, and he came over and put his hand on my shoulder. All eyes were on me, and I could feel myself starting to lose it; the shame and guilt were creeping in. This is exactly what I had wanted to avoid. I started to tear up. I didn't want to appear weak; I didn't want to break down. However, this time was different; something had shifted in me. Instead of averting my eyes and running away, I felt a deep sense of strength and an urge to hold my ground. I looked directly into the eyes of my dad's old teammates. I was expecting to see the eyes of judgment, but instead I saw something different. In their eyes, I saw nothing but love and respect for my father and for me. Tears were rolling down my checks as I stood my ground. Those around me shared their support and condolences. I then excused myself and slowly walked away.

I went up the bleachers and sat and looked out over the pool. I began to cry. There was nothing I could do to stop it. The tears just kept coming. After a little while, Lydon came up and sat beside me and put his arm over my shoulder. At that point I lost it even more. Lydon didn't say anything. He sat there beside me and let me cry.

CHAPTER 10

DESTINED TO THE SAME PATH

It is not the thing you fear that you must deal with,
it is the mother of the thing you fear. The very
thing that has given birth to the nightmare.

—David Whyte

MY TIME AT SMU WAS LIKE A SMALL RELEASE VALVE, BUT AS I CON-
TINUED THROUGH HIGH SCHOOL, I EXPERIENCED IMMENSE PRES-
SURE FROM EVERYTHING I HAD BEEN HOLDING IN. After returning
from the trip, I went right back to my old ways. I hardly talked
about my dad and his death, but I thought about it constantly.
On one hand, I thought about him in a way that put him up on
a pedestal; he had become a hero who I tried to emulate. On the
other hand, I had thoughts about him that stirred up a great deal
of fear inside me. I felt more and more that I was destined to
share his fate. I felt like I couldn't escape it.

I became a master of looking like I had it all together and acting as if I wasn't affected by the suicide. On the inside, though, I was a mess. As I got older, I could more fully comprehend the fact that my father had taken his own life. That understanding was like a giant weight on me. I felt like I couldn't get out from underneath it. At times it felt unbearable and inescapable.

Often when I was with extended family or family friends who knew my dad, they would see things in me reminiscent of him. They would say how much I looked like him or how similar certain mannerisms were. I remember once when Lydon and his wife Linda were in town visiting from Chicago. We had just finished dinner at our place when the conversation turned to embarrassing stories and things of that nature. My little sister took the liberty of sharing how I kept an empty water jug next to my bed so that at night I could pee in it to avoid having to get all the way up and walk to the bathroom. All of a sudden Lydon jumped in and said, "You're kidding me! Vernon used to do the very same thing when we were roommates." We all laughed at the strange and funny coincidence.

Later that night I thought it over and a familiar dark feeling crept up. *More proof that I am just like he was,* I thought. *There's no hiding it. There's no escape.* This sort of thing happened all the time, and whenever someone would say how much I was like him in this way or that, I would make a mental note of it and add it to my growing list of evidence as to why I would one day end up just like him.

Not only did we share many of the same mannerisms and tendencies, but I was constantly reminded of our shared physical traits as well. In many ways physically I take after my mom more than my dad. I inherited her leaner build and her blonde hair, blue eyes, and light complexion. However, anytime I looked in the mirror I was reminded I was my dad's son. I literally had a mark on my forehead to prove it.

I grew up hating my birthmarks. They were passed down to my sister and me from my dad. I had similar markings on my forehead as well as my chest, belly, and left calf. When I was young, I was often teased because of my odd markings. When others commented on my birthmarks, regardless of their intention, I interpreted it as negative. To me they were pointing out something that I felt almost constantly after my dad died, that there was something wrong with me, that I was marked or cursed in some way. This was just more evidence that I was seemingly destined to share my dad's fate.

My grades were less than stellar in high school; I wasn't in danger of flunking, but I certainly did not apply myself. When it came to my studies, like most people, there were subjects I naturally excelled in and others where I struggled. Subjects like math and science did not come easy to me, and I would often find myself giving up on homework or exams early and not giving it my all. I would give myself an out by telling myself, *That's okay. It's to be expected, given my childhood.* This not only happened in school but in all aspects of my life. If I got in trouble or got into a fight or drank too much, I had my excuse waiting for me. This wasn't something I shared with others, rather this dialogue went on in my head. It was something that made me feel okay with poor behavior or not giving my full effort.

I became exceptionally skilled at playing the victim. I made a lot of excuses and didn't hold myself accountable for my actions, which only reinforced my belief that there was something wrong with me and made me feel worse. When I look back on this time of my life and think about where I struggled and where I did well, it is clear that I had a very fixed idea of what I could and could not do. The areas I excelled in were mostly sports and physical activities, which I always felt I had a natural ability at. In those areas, I didn't mind putting in a lot of time and work with the hopes of getting better. In most of the rest of my life, however, I didn't bring that sort of proactive or growth mindset to the table.

As a result, this left me with a very narrow range of activities to participate in. I spent much of my time doing the things I was good at, like bodyboarding, soccer, and other sports, and very little time doing the things I wasn't good at, which was basically everything else. My comfort zone was small and shrinking. I missed out on so much of life because I was terrified of doing poorly or failing.

One night when I was in high school I was out drinking with my best friend, Matt. We had started drinking early with no real plan besides getting drunk and roaming around. Our evening consisted mostly of drinking, climbing trees or other tall things, and seeing who would jump from the highest point. I was terrified of heights, so Matt would typically win, but after a few drinks I could give him a run for his money. After a few hours of climbing, jumping, and exploring, we ended up sufficiently drunk and oddly enough in the courtyard of one of the local churches. I had walked by this church many times during the day, but had never entered the premises. Exhausted from all the climbing and jumping, we sat on a wooden bench in the courtyard; Matt reached into his backpack and pulled out a couple of beers.

We sat on the bench drinking and talking, and at one point the subject of my dad came up. Matt knew that my father had died when I was younger, only I told him he had been killed in a car accident. Aside from that, he knew very little. I had become skilled at avoiding questions or changing the subject whenever my dad came up. I was just about to change the subject when suddenly I felt the urge not to. I don't know what it was about that night, maybe the alcohol or the setting, but I decided to tell Matt the truth about my dad for a change. After all, he was my closest friend, and if I could trust anyone with this, it was him.

"My dad didn't die in a car crash," I told him as I looked down at the grass beneath our feet. My stomach was suddenly tense and I could feel my heart beating through my chest. "He killed himself."

Matt didn't say anything. We sat there in silence. There was dim light from the half moon above. I felt immense relief, followed by a surge of energy. I wanted to share more.

"He was an amazing swimmer from South Africa, a champion. He was a successful stockbroker. Had a beautiful, loving wife, and two healthy kids. I just don't understand. He had it all. And then, just like that, he ended it. He didn't look back; he just left us." I continued on from there. About how if he were still alive, we would have been rich and I would have grown up in La Jolla and Australia and South Africa, traveling around, living the perfect life. Matt listened intently.

Tears were rolling down my face at this point. Still looking down, I said, "But now he's gone and my mom, sister, and I are cursed. It wasn't supposed to be this way." As I spoke these words, I could feel the anger surging up from down deep, like electricity coursing through my body. My fists clenched tight and my jaw locked, I stood up vigorously and started to pace back and forth. I walked over to the church door, and beside it there was a stone statue of Jesus Christ. I grabbed ahold of the large statue and with all my strength pushed it to the ground, watching in enraged delight as it split into several pieces on the walkway below. All I wanted to do was hurt and break things. I wanted to blot out any light or love or life around me. *This isn't fair. It wasn't supposed to be like this,* I kept saying over and over in my head. Suddenly I collapsed onto my knees and broke down crying, my anger giving way to deep sadness and hopelessness.

Matt came over and sat next to me on the ground, putting his hand on my shoulder. "It's going to be okay," he said. "I've got your back."

"You want to know the most fucked-up thing about all of this?" I said, shaking my head back and forth. "One day when I can't take it anymore, I'm going to kill myself too. I know this for a fact. And there is nothing you or anyone else can do to stop it. It's my destiny."

"It doesn't have to be like that," Matt replied. "No matter what, I am here for you."

I smiled somewhat sarcastically, wiped the tears from my eyes and said, "I appreciate that, but there's nothing you can do to help me."

There were times during high school when I felt like I was falling down a deep, dark hole, and I didn't see a way out. The worst part of it was that I was alone, because I could hardly bring myself to talk to anyone about it. I often felt overwhelmed by the pressures and stresses of daily life.

There were periods when I would drink excessively. I kept a large bottle of vodka under my bed. I would drink before most social events and situations. Sometimes I would drink just to drink. I initially found great comfort in the way alcohol helped me feel numb—comfort that was very short-lived and often followed by excruciating feelings of despair. Often when I would drink or in the wake of drinking, the feelings of anger and sadness that I had for my father and why he did what he did would rise to the surface. There were times when I became so overwhelmed by these feelings that I wanted to kill myself. I felt such a sense of relief while contemplating suicide. *It would be so nice just to end all this,* I'd think to myself.

There were times while thinking about suicide when I felt a surge of power. I felt like a martyr. I would sit in my room and drink late into the night and imagine how my dad would have felt before taking his life. I meditated on this, became obsessed with it. There was a power and confidence there, a sense of having total control over your life and your destiny. It was a feeling of contempt for the world, of being above it all. I would smile and think to myself, *Well, life, if you aren't going to cooperate with me, then fuck you. I'm out of here. Fuck you and fuck everyone else.* I fed off these dark thoughts. They made me feel alive and jacked. I would get goose bumps and the hairs on my body would stand up.

I also felt there was honor in following in my dad's footsteps. I imagined killing myself and then meeting my dad in the afterlife.

There the two of us would swim and explore our new world, and laugh about those suckers stuck back in the hell that we called earth.

I can remember one night in particular; it was late and I sat in my room drinking by myself. I had been recovering from a knee injury which had kept me out of the water and away from bodyboarding for several weeks. Anytime I was away from bodyboarding, I struggled. I sat and stared at the picture of my dad on the wall. All I wanted to do was be with him. And in that moment, I felt ready to fulfill my destiny.

There was just one question. How would I do it? I thought to myself, *I could do what my dad did. Only, it's 2 o'clock in the morning. If I turn the car on, Mom will wake up. Plus, there's something about carbon monoxide poisoning that seems a little soft. Something else then, but what?* I thought about taking pills and just drifting off into the darkness. That seemed appealing but soft as well. I didn't like guns, so that was off the table. Cutting was out too, because I hated blood and got queasy at the idea of it. *What about something to do with nature, with the ocean? I've got it! I'll just swim straight out into the ocean as far as I can go. I'll either drown or get attacked by a shark. Yes, that's the way to do it.*

At the time, our house was within walking distance of the beach. My room was a little studio/laundry room, which had a separate entrance, making it easy for me to come and go as I pleased. I stood up and took one last swig of vodka, opened the sliding glass door, and stepped out into the night. It was cold and windy and the sky was clear.

I pulled my hooded sweatshirt over my head and made my way quietly and stealthily down our driveway so as not to wake my mom or sister. As I walked, I heard a little voice ask in the back of my mind, *What are you doing? You can't do this. What about your mom and sister?*

No, not now. Stay focused. You have a job to do, another more powerful voice said.

I continued to walk with swiftness and determination down the road toward the beach. There was no one around. As I approached the long staircase which led down the bluff to the sand, I felt the chill and resistance of the cold wind howling onshore. I initially put my head down and folded my arms across my chest to stay warm. I arrived at the top of the staircase and looked out over the ocean. My stomach dropped. The ocean looked fierce and chaotic. Huge stormy waves roared in from as far as I could see under the dim light of the crescent moon. The waves and the wind were remnants of a winter storm that had recently passed through. I hadn't anticipated these conditions.

Then I reminded myself that this was a powerful defiant act, so I stood tall and faced the wind. I looked up at the clear night sky and the stars above and said to myself, *I'll see you soon.* Like a warrior heading into battle, I made my way down the steps with focus and intensity. The roar of the waves grew louder as I walked down the stairs. When I got down to the sand, I kicked my shoes off and stripped down to my underwear. I shivered as I walked toward the water, feeling the cold wet sand beneath my feet. The tide was low and the walk seemed to take forever. I gasped as a small wave rushed cold water in over my feet. It was freezing. I paused for a moment, but then doubled down my focus and proceeded to march into the great Pacific. As I went deeper, I could feel the power of the waves and the current on this stormy night.

I struggled to move ahead through the waves, and kept getting pushed back. I was about waist deep and getting ready to dive under and start swimming. I paused and turned around to face the beach. Somewhere in the back of my mind I was hoping someone was going to be there. There was no one. I turned around to face the ocean, took a deep breath, and dove under the next wave. The cold water felt like pins and needles. With the shock of the cold, I jumped back to my feet and gasped for air. One after another the waves pushed me back toward shore. I dove under two more waves. My forehead ached from the cold. I couldn't get through it. I was no match for this.

I stopped and stood shivering violently. And suddenly I felt different. I felt sober. And instead of feeling power, I felt remorse. I imagined my mom and my sister waking up the next morning and finding my room empty. I imagined what they would go through when they found my body. I thought about my friends and extended family and what it would be like for them. I stood there just feeling the intensity of the cold as wave after wave rushed into me. I looked around at the fierce but beautiful ocean and then up at the starry sky.

I put my hands down and felt the surface of the water as it flowed all around me. I thought about my dad's ashes being spread in the ocean. The idea that I had to die in order to be back with him now felt absurd. He was right here with me. My dad and the ocean were one. I felt his presence, and I couldn't help but think that he was there in the storm and in the waves that had pushed me back to my senses, as if to say, *Not today, Sebastian. This isn't your time.*

It had become painfully clear that my way of coping with my dad's suicide—protecting myself by running away from the pain—was no longer working. Standing there so close to the edge, shaking in the cold, I thought to myself, *How the hell did I get here? What am I doing? I need to find a way to get past this.* I didn't know how it would happen, but it was clear to me that something had to change.

CHAPTER 11

CHANGE IN PERSPECTIVE

Perhaps the truth depends on a walk around the lake.

—Wallace Stevens

The following year, when I was 17 years old, I had the opportunity to return to Australia for the first time since I was 5. Being a senior in high school, I was surprised that my mom allowed this trip. I wasn't the best student, and I would be missing three weeks of school. I think my mom knew that going back to Australia would be very important for me. There were three places around the world which held significance in terms of connection to my dad. They also happened to be his three favorite cities: La Jolla, California, where I had grown up and had the most memories of my dad; Cape Town, South Africa, the place of my dad's birth and where he had grown up (I had only visited once when I was very young); and Perth, Australia, the place where he died. I held these places in a sacred reverence. This was my chance to go back and reconnect with Perth and the beautiful country of Australia.

On the surface, it was my dream trip. Even though I had only lived in Australia for a short time when I was younger, I felt a strong connection to the country. Our family had stayed in touch with the Kennedys over the years, and I viewed them as our extended family overseas. I was looking forward to reconnecting with them after so long. During the weeks before the trip, it was all I could talk about or think about. While I was excited for the adventure, part of me was terrified. For the first two weeks of the trip I was scheduled to stay in Perth with the Kennedys. They lived just a few blocks from where my dad had died.

I knew I was going to have to face my dad's suicide; there was no avoiding it. While I was scared, a part of me was beginning to emerge that wanted to confront the past. I knew that I couldn't run away forever.

The Kennedys, John David and Sara, were originally from Johannesburg, South Africa. John David and my father were the same age. And, like my father, John David, or JD, as we called him, was one of the best young swimmers in South Africa at the time. As a boy, my dad would travel to Johannesburg from Cape Town each winter to swim and train for the season, because at the time Cape Town didn't have a heated pool. John David's family was kind enough to host my dad each winter. It was over years of training together that my dad and JD became close friends. When my dad went off to the United States to swim for SMU, John David stayed in South Africa. JD later married his sweetheart, Sara, and they had two sons, John Jr. and Mark. Their family eventually emigrated from Johannesburg, South Africa, to Perth, Australia, in the late '70s. All the while, our families stayed in close touch.

I made the long trip from San Diego to Perth (via Los Angeles, Auckland, and Brisbane), and when I arrived in the afternoon I was completely exhausted, both mentally and physically. I remember being hit by the intense summer heat as I left the cool air-conditioned airport terminal. With the combination of the jet lag and the heat, I felt like I had taken several sleeping pills and then was put into a sauna.

Sara picked me up from the airport. She was older than my mom, but she was so energetic and full of life. I was struck by her incredibly positive spirit. Although I hadn't seen her since I was five years old, she treated me like family from the moment I arrived. I was ready to crawl into bed, but Sara was insistent that I stay up until the sun set in order to adjust to Perth time more quickly. She had a series of little adventures to keep me going until nightfall. I gazed out the car window in wonder at the natural beauty of Perth and the surrounding land as Sara gave me a brief tour of the area. We made our way to a local golf course, which was home to several kangaroos. It was incredible to watch the strange creatures move about the green, and even stranger that the golfers played through, paying little attention to them.

I was captivated by this beautiful place and its extraordinary animals. After the golf course, we went down to Scarborough Beach, which Sara explained was my dad's favorite beach in Perth. I felt a tinge of anxiety as she mentioned his name. To my relief she left it at that, and my attention was drawn back to the natural beauty of the Indian Ocean. With the stunning blue-green water in contrast to the bright white sand, I understood why he was so drawn to it. I had vague memories of having been there before, but that seemed as if it was a different lifetime. Being uncomfortably warm and sleep deprived only added to the surreal nature of the experience.

I stayed awake until sunset, but just barely, and went to bed early that evening. I slept like a rock, and the next morning I awoke to meet John David. He had been working the evening before and only got back after I had gone to bed. He was quiet and humble and it was clear he was a warm and caring person. After breakfast the two of us went out on a walk around the suburb of Mount Pleasant where they lived. Sara said she thought it would be a good idea for the two of us to have some alone time.

We made our way down toward the Canning River. I was captivated by the pristine beauty of Perth, by how clear the sky was and how fresh the air was. Fluffy white clouds were slowly floating by as we walked through the neighborhood. They were the kind of clouds that seemed like you could reach up and pluck them from the sky.

We walked for a while, making small talk about the weather and the different types of flora and fauna in the area. I mentioned that Perth felt very similar to back home.

"It's amazing how quiet it is here. It seems just like Southern California, but with a fraction of the people," I said as we crossed what seemed like a major road, only without traffic in either direction. Once on the other side, we made our way to the walking path along the river. I looked over at John David, who was smiling as he looked down toward the ground.

He then let out a soft chuckle and said, "Your father would go on and on about how uncrowded it was here compared to San

Diego." I could feel my chest tighten as soon as the word "father" came out of his mouth. *Here we go,* I thought to myself. This, surely, was when my pleasant trip would turn south.

He went on, "When you all were living in Melbourne, your dad came out here to visit for a week before bringing your mom, sister, and you along. The first day he was here, he wanted to make the drive into downtown during rush hour. He had nothing to do downtown; he just wanted to experience rush-hour traffic. Your dad was so set on it that I obliged," he said, looking at me with a smile. "At the time there was hardly any rush-hour traffic, and your dad was ecstatic throughout the short drive. He kept saying, 'Can you believe this! No rush-hour traffic. This is incredible!' I had never seen someone so excited about a lack of traffic. I often think about that while driving downtown."

I was silent for a moment and then said, "Yeah, I remember Mom telling me about how much he hated the traffic in San Diego."

We continued for a few minutes without saying anything. Then John David shared how he had met my dad and all about their time growing up in South Africa together. Being caught up in the flow of the conversation, I found myself becoming less nervous and more curious. I asked about what my dad was like when they were growing up. "He was a great friend. And one hell of a competitor. I have never met anyone with the willpower and determination that he had. It served him very well as a swimmer," John David explained.

He went on to talk more about the relationship they had built over the years and that no matter how far away they were living from each other, they maintained a strong friendship. "I was completely shocked when I heard he had died. It was one of the most difficult days of my life," he said, shaking his head and looking downward. "He was such a special man. He meant a great deal to us all. His death was terrible on the boys," referring to his sons John and Mark, who were in their late teens at the time, "They looked up to him so much." There were so many questions I wanted to ask and so much I wanted to say, but I didn't.

What he went on to say would change my life forever. "Seb, I'm not sure if you know this, but my father committed suicide when I was a boy." I remember that moment like it was yesterday. "My father had been going through some difficult times; he had been drinking heavily and had been fighting with my mother a lot.

"One morning I overheard the two of them fighting, which wasn't out of the ordinary, only it sounded more intense than usual. I walked into the room to intervene and found my father aiming a pistol at my mother and screaming at her. I didn't know what to do, so I stepped in front of her to shield her. As soon as I did, my father turned the gun on himself and pulled the trigger."

I listened in disbelief as John David continued, "I was 15 years old and we were living in Johannesburg at the time. This was at a time when people didn't talk about mental health issues, and they certainly didn't talk about suicide. One of the most difficult parts for me was that my family never spoke about it. Our family and neighborhood was close-knit, and although everyone knew what had happened to my father, it was not up for discussion. Suicide was completely taboo. While we didn't talk about it, I could certainly feel it. The shame and stigma around his suicide was palpable. I began to think there was something wrong with me by association.

"It took me a very long time to talk about what had happened that day. I think those years of having to keep that part of my past buried took a big toll."

There was a moment of silence as we continued to walk slowly along the path. I didn't know what to say; there was so much to process. I felt a familiar sadness and empathy for what John David had been through. I also felt, for the first time in my life, that I was in a safe place to share my experience and that I would be met with understanding. I now had the chance to talk with someone who knew what it was like. I didn't feel alone. And then a curious thing happened. I felt that I not only had permission to talk about my dad's death, but that I wanted to. JD had the courage to start the conversation, and this allowed me to open up about something I desperately needed to.

There, walking along the banks of the river, I spoke about my father's death with a sense of openness and freedom I hadn't experienced before. Up until that point, the few times I had spoken about my dad's suicide had been from a place of shame and fear. I confessed that, like John David, I hadn't been able to talk about my dad's death because of the intense stigma I felt from others and from my own shame. I felt like no one would understand me. I shared my fear that if I opened up, it would allow all the dark thoughts to surface—thoughts and feelings that I had spent so long running away from. I confided that I didn't know if I could handle it. And even though it was frightening for me, with every word I spoke I felt lighter.

We took a rest on a wooden bench overlooking the river. I remember breathing more easily and deeply than I had in quite some time. It was as if I had been carrying around a backpack full of rocks and I was finally able to shed some of the weight. I remember being fully tuned in to the beauty of the present moment, to the sights, sounds, and scents all around me. It felt like I was back home in the ocean.

We sat taking in the scenery, and then John David turned to me and said, "You know, Seb, your dad was an incredible man. His death took such a toll on all of us who were close to him, especially you and your family. And while it was a great loss, I want you to know that this event in your past does not *have* to dictate your life. We all go through difficult times at one point or another. It can be so easy to use past difficulties as an excuse to make poor decisions in the present, to play the victim and blame life. Nothing that happened in the past has the power to control the decisions you make right now."

I listened intently as he went on to say, "I spent years running away from my father's death. I've learned that running away is not only ineffective, it's impossible. Until we turn to face what we're afraid of, it will always haunt us. If there is one thing I can pass along to you, it would be to stop running. And who knows? What you are seeking may just come to you."

I took a deep breath as I looked out over the flowing water. As I sat in the silence taking in what he shared, I saw that even more powerful than his words, John David was living proof of that realization. Here was someone who had gone through a very traumatic experience as a youth but didn't let that control or dictate his life. He had grown into a very grounded and successful person. This was my first glimmer of realizing that my past did not have total control over my life, that it did not control my destiny.

This conversation with John David allowed me to look at my father's death in a different light. I thought to myself, *If the past can't control me, why do I have to fear it? And if I don't fear it, I can confront it and learn from it.* That was the moment I began to look at my father's life and death as my teacher. I went from running away from my fears to turning and facing them.

After a few minutes of silence, we made our way back toward the house. We continued the conversation as we walked, in between enjoying stretches of peaceful silence. As our walk along the river came to an end, I remember feeling so light and full of energy.

That was the first of many conversations I had about my father and my past on that trip. It wasn't all about suicide and loss. I heard JD and Sara share many wonderful stories and memories they had of my father. All of it, the good and the bad, was medicine for me.

After spending several days in Perth, we drove south along the coast to a town called Margaret River. The land and coastline near Margaret River had some of the most beautiful scenery I had ever seen. The region is also home to some of the best surf spots in the world, so naturally I took to it right away. We arrived in the afternoon to our beautiful little condo rental, which was just a few minutes' walk from Smith's Beach. I had heard it was a stunning secluded beach with white sand and crystal-clear water. I quickly unpacked and made my way down to the beach to take a dip.

The beach was breathtaking. The sand was so fine that it made a squeaky noise with every step I took as I made my way toward the water. It was summertime, and the waves were almost nonexistent, which gave the Indian Ocean a lake-like feel. I took a deep breath as I made my way into the cool, clear water. After a few steps the water was up past my waist. I took a deep breath and dove in. I opened my eyes and swam deeper, following the sand as it continued downward. After a few strokes, I stopped and looked at the different shades of blue and green all around me. It felt oddly familiar. It felt just like the dream I had had years before. Only, instead of feeling panicked that my dad had abandoned me, I had the sense that he was there in some way; he was there to guide me.

For some time I continued swimming up to the surface and then diving back down, experiencing the magic of the underwater world. Eventually I made my way back to the shore and sat on the sand, gazing out on the horizon. I thought back on my life since my dad's death. I thought about the ups and the downs and then contemplated what John David had shared with me just days before. I felt reborn, like I was looking at the world from a fresh perspective. And I had the sense that there was a great opportunity before me.

Prior to my trip to Australia I had felt destined to go down the same grim path as my dad. I was going through life ready and willing to hit the eject button if I happened to find myself in a situation I couldn't handle. There on the beach I wondered, *Perhaps it isn't too late for me. Maybe there is another way to live.* Looking out at the beauty all around me, I set an intention to stop running away from my past. I vowed to take every opportunity I could to learn about my father and what had happened to him. I wanted to understand, as much as possible, why he took his own life and what lessons I could learn from it.

My time in Australia was my impetus for setting out on a journey to uncover my father's story. My plan was to search out the people who knew him best and gather all the stories and information I could to figure out why he committed suicide and what I could learn from it. It was my personal research project. My goal was to put the pieces of this puzzle back together. I was just about to graduate high school, and with my bodyboarding career moving forward, I'd be able to combine my travel for bodyboarding with my personal research project on my dad.

CHAPTER 12

THE QUEST

Security is mostly a superstition. It does not exist in nature, nor do the children of men as a whole experience it. Avoiding danger is no safer in the long run than outright exposure. Life is either a daring adventure, or nothing.

—Helen Keller

ON THE LONG FLIGHT BACK FROM AUSTRALIA I MADE A LIST OF EVERYONE I KNEW WHO HAD SPENT SIGNIFICANT TIME WITH MY DAD AND COULD SHARE THEIR PERSPECTIVE. I listed the family and friends I knew of who grew up with him in South Africa, who were now spread out in different parts of the world. I wrote down the names of those who went to college with him and those who had worked with him and knew him from a business perspective.

I wrote down the questions I wanted to ask. Questions about my dad that I wanted to learn more about, such as: What was he like as a friend/teammate/business partner? What was he most passionate about? What were his strengths? What were his weaknesses or flaws? Other questions were focused around his suicide. Questions like: What were the core reasons he ended his life? How could he have gone from someone of so much promise and confidence to one of desperation and fear? Was there something specific that happened along his path? Was it one thing or many? And once I understood what those things were, could they be avoided?

I certainly didn't want to make the same mistakes he had. While I had a basic understanding of some of those questions, I knew surprisingly little about my father and what had happened to him. I had done an excellent job of evading this topic in the past.

In terms of my "research," I knew the questions and answers would vary depending on each person's relationship with my dad. Overall, I had a clear idea of what my mission was: with each friend, family member, teammate, or co-worker I had the opportunity to speak with, there was the possibility of uncovering a little more of this mystery. I went into this journey with the mindset of a detective. I would be like Hansel and Gretel following breadcrumbs along the way to my destination. What was my destination exactly? To uncover the mystery behind my father's suicide and learn from it.

While I desperately wanted to come away from this research understanding why he took his own life, I understood that I'd never be able to know the complete story. That information and that story died along with my dad. Although I knew there were some things I would never fully understand, I was beginning to see that there was a great deal for me to learn. A great deal that my father could teach me.

When I got back from Australia, my enthusiasm was high and I was excited to start checking the names off my list. That is, until

I thought of another name to help me out on this journey, an obvious one which I had initially overlooked somehow: my mom. Suddenly this mission became considerably more intimidating. I was okay (or so I imagined) with the level of discomfort and vulnerability it would take to reach out to the people on my list. Most of them I didn't know very well, and many were in far-off places. However, the idea of talking to my mom about this didn't sit well, not at all. Suddenly, things got real; this wasn't going to be a walk in the park. I began to realize there was no possible way to complete this mission without confronting one of my biggest fears. The thought of having that conversation with her, which I imagined would bring up many dark and painful memories, tortured me. I could feel the fear and weight of everything begin to creep back upon me, and my enthusiasm and confidence waned. This was not going to be easy.

When I first got back and told my mom and sister about the trip, I nearly told them about my life-changing conversation with John David, but I didn't. My mom and sister seemed to be doing well and I didn't want to bring all this old stuff back up. I did what I typically do: I thought about how I would have the conversation and when the right time would be, but I didn't act. *I'll do it tomorrow,* I thought. Tomorrow came and went, and then days turned to weeks and weeks to months. I thought a lot about having this conversation with my mom, but continued to avoid it. I rationalized that perhaps it would make more sense to start somewhere a little easier on my list. So, I decided to get together with a close family friend named Reed Thompson who lived in the area.

Reed was a tall and distinguished-looking man who was in his late sixties. He had graying hair and glasses and reminded me of Steve Martin. Plus, he had a great sense of humor. I had known Reed my entire life. He had been my dad's business partner for many years and knew him well, both personally and professionally. I was curious to hear Reed's take on my dad, especially from a business perspective. Reed, still working as a stockbroker, had a busy schedule but made time to get together with me for dinner later that week.

We met at a nice Thai restaurant in town. It was crowded when we arrived, but our booth made the space feel more private. We ate and drank and caught up with each other. It took me nearly the entire dinner to build up the courage to ask about my dad. Reed was slightly taken aback when I finally broached the subject, but said he expected me to reach out at some point. He proceeded to jump right in, as if he had been waiting and ready to do so. While Reed had initially met my dad through business, it was clear they had cultivated a deep friendship. Also, Reed knew a surprising amount about my dad's swimming career, and I came to learn that my dad even helped coach his son through high school swim team.

"Your dad was an absolute beast in the water. One afternoon he was down at Windansea watching the sunset. The lifeguards had gone off duty and he noticed a couple of swimmers getting pulled out in a large rip current. Having been a lifeguard in South Africa growing up and being the swimmer he is, he just bolted out there and saved both of them like it was nothing, without swim fins or anything. The local paper even did a story on the rescue."

I hadn't heard any of this before. I was riveted. "That's wild!" I said. "Wait, he was a lifeguard in South Africa? I didn't know that," I said, surprised.

"You didn't know he was a lifeguard? Your mom must have told you about that," he replied with a look of shock on his face.

"I don't think I knew that," I replied. After saying this, I realized perhaps she or someone else did tell me, and maybe I was so shut down to hearing about my dad that I didn't remember.

"Yes, he was a lifeguard. And a hell of a one from what I heard. He worked at Clifton 4th Beach in Cape Town. That was his favorite beach in the world. He was always comparing the beaches here to Clifton's."

"Clifton 4th Beach, huh." I nodded and made a mental note to look up the beach.

Reed continued with a smile, "You know, it's funny, Seb, after seeing the article in the paper I remember walking up to your dad in our office the next day and asking, "Gee, you didn't have swim fins or a rescue buoy. Weren't you worried that people panicking like that could pull you under and drown you?" Your dad looked me square in the eyes and with a little smirk he said, "Reed, nobody could drown me." Reed was smiling, clearly still amused by my dad's reply. He went on, "And you know something, Seb, as arrogant as that sounded, there was just something about your dad that I believed him without a shadow of a doubt."

Reed went on to describe the intensity that he brought not only to his swimming but to work as well. "He trained and worked harder than anyone I knew; it didn't matter whether he was swimming or making cold calls. He was an animal. Your dad was an amazing businessman and salesman; he was a master at creating and developing relationships." Reed continued, "While he was probably the most driven, he was also one of the most stubborn people I ever knew. When obstacles got in his way, he would put his head down and fight through them. He never backed down."

I sat there and listened, completely fascinated by what Reed was sharing. "I believe what set Vernon apart," he continued, "was his ability to take what made him successful as a world-class swimmer and apply those principles to his business. In the pool, he would train fiercely and relentlessly. He had incredible willpower and could push past many physical and mental limitations. When other people would become discouraged or quit, your dad kept charging forward. He could make cold call after cold call, and the rejection wouldn't faze him at all, or at least he didn't seem fazed. He would just keep on driving toward his financial goals no differently than he would toward the finish line."

"What do you think was his motivation in business? What drove him?" I asked.

Reed replied without hesitation, "The same thing that motivated him in swimming. He always wanted to be the very best. He wanted to be the top broker in our office. He wanted to have the most clients and the best clients. He wanted to make the most money. He wanted to be number one."

I nodded in understanding. "Well, that all sounds pretty good. It sounds like he had plenty of drive and the skills to get what he wanted. What do you think were some of his weaknesses then?" I said, curious to dig a little deeper.

"That's a good question, Seb." Reed paused to process my inquiry. "I think his challenges were similar to what made him great. Sometimes his stubbornness got the better of him."

We talked for hours that night. I was so focused on the conversation that I didn't even notice we were the last ones in the restaurant. We continued talking as we walked out into the cool night air. We were out in the parking lot when we got to the subject of his suicide. Reed got a little teary-eyed as he spoke about my dad's death. He seemed to be feeling a mix of sadness and anger as he reflected. "I still think about your dad quite often. He was one of my best friends, and I loved him like a brother. But sometimes I get so pissed when I think about what he put you all through." Reed paused and shook his head, looking down. After a few moments, his demeanor changed. He went on to share how incredibly strong my mom had been during those rough times and how fortunate my sister and I are to have her. I felt proud and grateful to have her as a mother, but I also felt a tension in my stomach and jaw. I thought about what Reed had said just moments before. I thought about the hell my dad put us through. I could feel my own anger and frustration rising up.

"Thanks for reaching out, Seb. Let's do it again soon," Reed said with his arms spread wide, I was suddenly pulled out of my head and into the present moment. I gave Reed a hug and thanked him.

I went home that night and straight to my room. I paced back and forth, still buzzing from our conversation. There was so much to process, but mostly I felt angry. I was acutely aware of how selfish my dad had been in many ways. With my fists clenched, I started to unleash punch after punch on my pillows and mattress. I kept going until I collapsed in exhaustion on the floor. I sat with my head in my hands and broke down crying. It felt cathartic to be there, feeling what was coming up and not trying to numb it, suppress it, or be anyplace else. I was on a new path and beginning to live by John David's wise words from our conversation in Australia; I was beginning to face my fears.

A few days later I followed up with Reed, and we agreed to get together once a month or so to catch up and continue the conversation. Those meetings gave me a chance to ask more questions and practice continuing to step into my long-neglected anger and sadness. Those conversations also gave me momentum to continue with my list and reach out to others.

Over the course of the next year I connected with many of the people on my list in person when possible; others I spoke to by phone, and some via email. I learned something different from everyone that I spoke with. It also became apparent that regardless of who I spoke with or their relationship with my dad, similar themes and patterns about my dad emerged. I was beginning to get a better sense of what my dad was like and was starting to develop a hypothesis of why he had taken his own life. The pieces of the puzzle were beginning to come together.

Not long after connecting with Reed I had a chance to speak with Richard Bonney. Richard and his wife at the time, Derelynn Bonney, were two of my parents' closest friends in San Diego. Similar to my dad, Richard was one of a handful of South African swimmers recruited by SMU in the '60s and '70s. He had known my dad for many years and from a variety of perspectives. Richard shared with me how my dad's intensity and focus bordered on obsession with whatever he put his mind to.

"We (your mom, dad, Derelynn, and I) would always go out Saturday nights. It was a long-standing tradition before you were born. We would often mix it up, sometimes going out in La Jolla, other times going to Mission Beach or downtown. But each year, as the La Jolla Rough Water Swim or other races got closer, your dad would become more and more rigid in terms of where he would go and where he wouldn't. When a race was coming up, it was as if he blocked out all other distractions and solely focused on the race and, more specifically, on winning.

"It was like clockwork. The La Jolla Rough Water Swim was in early September, and by August of each year he would become a full-on germophobe, doing everything possible to avoid feeling less than perfect on race day. Eventually there was only one restaurant he felt comfortable going to. It was as if in everything he did, he had the finish line in mind.

"He trained like a madman. Every day he would swim the course of the race completely using the butterfly stroke, which is nearly unheard of for that type of distance. During the actual race, he swam freestyle, of course, but that was his unique way of preparing for the race. Leading up to the race, he recorded his swim times, weight, what he ate, and how he felt that day on a scale from 1 to 10." Richard chuckled as he shared this with me one afternoon over lunch. He continued, "We all gave him a hard time for it and he certainly knew he was going a bit overboard, but that never stopped him. And, if winning was his goal, what he did certainly worked. From what I remember, he won the La Jolla Rough Water Swim each year he entered. He certainly won his age group every time, and in his midthirties and forties would often win the younger age group, beating men in their twenties."

My time with Richard was very helpful in giving me insight into the early years of my parents' relationship. During the conversation, I felt waves of feeling both proud and nervous. I was proud to learn more about my dad's persistence and greatness as a swimmer. I felt tinges of fear hearing about his quirks and peculiarities around competition and winning. I saw many similarities to how I approached my own life, especially when it came to bodyboarding.

I continued to learn about my dad through regular conversations with my godfather, Lydon. He had done a great job of checking in with me over the years. We had developed quite a bond, especially after our trip to SMU. We spoke by phone and via email, as he lived in Chicago. On occasion when he was in San Diego on business, we would get together in person. The following is from an email thread between Lydon and me that helped me to understand more about my dad and gave insight into his college years.

We were roommates when he first came to SMU. While he was an intense competitor in the water, on land he was one of the nicest guys I'd ever met. We developed a great friendship during our time at school. During summer vacation, he would often come with me to train in Fort Lauderdale, Florida, rather than go all the way back home to Cape Town. We trained in the International Swimming Hall of Fame Pool with Olympic swimmer and future U.S. Olympic coach, Jack Nelson.

Vernon loved to train long hours, almost exclusively doing the butterfly, which was certainly unique. Most butterfly swimmers mix up their workouts with freestyle and other strokes, in order to tolerate the laps and mileage. Butterfly is the most difficult stroke to master, but Vernon pushed himself harder than any other by insisting on this training regimen.

Typically butterfly swimmers kick twice per butterfly stroke. Your dad had developed an unorthodox one-kick-per-stroke technique. His reasoning was that he could manage further distances and train longer with his technique. The trade-off was a loss of absolute speed in shorter races, such as the 100-meter fly. Coach Nelson tried to win him over to the universally accepted two-kicks-per-stroke approach, even after he went faster in a time trial. Vernon showed absolute insistence on only using one kick per butterfly stroke. Ultimately, Coach Nelson smiled and gave in to Vernon's firm but stubborn commitment to "his way."

Whether in the pool, at school, or socializing, Vernon choose to be distinctive and unique. He was not a follower, but very independent and apparently self-sufficient in his needs. Conformity was the last thing on his mind, and it didn't impact how he did things. If questioned, he would either smile or ignore the logic of others or the crowd.

With every conversation, I was learning something new about my dad. I was beginning to put the pieces of the puzzle together, and my hypothesis for why he had committed suicide as well as what I could learn from it was becoming clearer. With each conversation, I was becoming more comfortable with talking about my dad and his death. It took me about a year and dozens of other conversations to finally gain the courage to talk to my mom.

CHAPTER 13

THE POSTCARD

*Everything is shown up by being exposed to the light,
and whatever is exposed to the light itself becomes
light.*

—Saint Paul

IT WAS THE SUMMER OF 2003, 13 YEARS AFTER MY DAD'S DEATH.
I was 19 years old and had been out of high school for a year.
During that year, I had traveled a ton for bodyboarding. I spent
a good portion of that winter in Hawaii and the spring in South
America. I was back living at home with my mom and sister for
the summer between surf trips.

The year before, we had moved from our rental near the beach
a few miles inland to a townhouse in Solana Beach. We had been
renting ever since my dad died. Now, we were in a much better
place financially, and with the help of my grandpa Fred (my mom's
dad), my mom was able to buy a two-bedroom townhouse. My
mom had the master bedroom and Tanasa, who was 15 years old
and in high school at the time, got the other bedroom. I set up a

makeshift room in part of the garage downstairs for when I was in town. It wasn't anything too fancy, but it was perfect for my needs. I had a bed and dresser and some space for surfing and bodyboarding gear. We hung a divider between my living space and the rest of the garage, which was piled with old boxes—the contents of which were remnants of a life and the photos, memories, and other things we had many years ago when we lived in a much bigger house.

Being home for the summer, I picked up a job bussing tables in the evenings at a local restaurant to save for my travels and to supplement the meager income I made as a professional bodyboarder. I was gearing up for a series of trips to Mexico and Central America in the late summer and fall, and then back to Hawaii that winter. I knew that being at home during this time was the perfect opportunity to start the conversation with my mom.

I chose a calm weekend afternoon while my sister was away. I felt nervous and tense going into it. It felt like I was getting ready to dig out a deep splinter I had been avoiding for some time. My mom and I had just finished lunch, and as we were cleaning up, I asked, "Mom, there's something I want to talk with you about. Do you have some time?"

"Of course," she said, her words calm, but I could see the concern in her eyes. We sat down at the dining-room table. "What is it?" she asked. I could hear the tension in her voice. The words "There's something I want to talk with you about" weren't typically associated with anything good in our family.

"Well, I've been thinking a lot about this, and I want to talk about Dad." I could see her body tighten as I mentioned him.

"Okay," she said hesitantly.

"When I was in Australia last year, I had the chance to talk with John David about Dad's suicide and everything." As I spoke, it occurred to me that I had said the word "suicide" in front of my mom for perhaps the first time ever. I continued, "And, it was incredibly helpful. Actually, it was more than that; it was life-changing. The conversations I had with him helped shift my perspective on the whole thing. I've realized I don't want to run away from this any longer. I want to talk about it and I want to see if there is something I can learn from it."

She smiled a meager half smile and replied, "I'm happy that you had the chance to talk with John David. Of course we can talk about it." While it was difficult to begin, once the conversation got underway I didn't feel anxious anymore. I didn't feel comfortable either; I felt alive.

As our conversation began to gain steam, my curiosity grew and I started asking about all sorts of things. We covered a lot of ground, and it was fascinating to get her perspective on things. Some of it brought back wonderful memories for my mom and some if it brought back hellish memories.

As I listened, I was struck by how similar themes came up from conversations I'd had about my dad with others. I asked what she considered his best qualities and those that hindered him. My mom helped me gain more clarity on how obsessed my dad was with his goals. This was, from her perspective, both a strength and a weakness.

She explained how his obsession with goals played a central role in his life and at times seemed to take him over completely.

Whether they were financial goals or fitness/swimming-related, he was always focused on accomplishing the next goal, on reaching the finish line. As an example, she went on to tell me that he always had a very specific vision for how things were supposed to be in terms of their living situation. He had envisioned this utopia, which he was constantly searching for. It was a place where they could have a big house near the beach, where the weather was wonderful like San Diego, Cape Town, or Perth, but somewhere that wasn't too densely populated and didn't have much traffic. This place also had to be safe enough for young children to be raised well, and it needed to have a thriving economy that would be able to provide a high-paying job. After my mom explained this, we both had a little chuckle; even at the idealistic age of 19, that seemed like a fantasy to me.

My mom shared that while those lofty goals and vision of achieving perfection drove him to achieve a great deal, he was rarely satisfied with what he had. At least not for long. Once he achieved his goal, he was on to the next thing without taking the time to enjoy what he had. In the end, he couldn't seem to find what he was looking for.

The conversation twisted and turned, and we eventually got to his suicide. I knew the general story, but not the details. She shared with me her experience of the night she was woken up at 2 a.m. with the call from Dad's cousin Tim in Australia, telling her the news. She trembled as she recounted the event. Even though all this had happened many years ago, she recounted it just like it was yesterday. It became clear that my mom hadn't given herself the chance (or wasn't able) to process the loss of my dad, her late husband. She spoke about the days and weeks that followed and how overwhelmed she was. I had always had a great deal of respect for my mom and how much she overcame. Hearing things from her perspective made me very aware of how incredibly strong she was.

After hearing about that night and the chaos that followed, I wanted to step back and learn more about the months leading up to his suicide. My intention was to ease the tension a bit, but things only got more intense. When I started to ask questions to gain clarity around parts of the story that were fuzzy, specifically around what had happened when we moved back to the United States from Australia, it was as if she went right back to that time. Her face became flush and her body tense.

I listened intently as she spoke about her decision to stay in San Diego with my sister and me, and not return to Australia with my dad. "It was one of the hardest decisions I've ever made. After he died, I couldn't help but wonder if things would have been different. What if I had made the decision for us to go back to Australia with him? You would still have a dad. It should have been different. I should have gone back to support him." I was taken aback. All these years later, and there was still an incredible amount of guilt (and blaming herself) for not going with him. We sat in silence and I watched as a few tears rolled down her face.

I could feel the weight of what my mom had been carrying for all these years, and I began to feel a surge of anger. "No, Mom," I said, shaking my head. "This was not your fault. You did everything you could do." I thought about what I'd say to my dad if he was here in the room. Maybe it was good that he was dead, because I was ready to kill him. *How could he have done this? How could he have put my mom through this, put us through this?* I thought to myself with my fists and jaw clenched. I looked over at my mom, and all I wanted to do was help her and take away her pain. I took a deep breath and said, "Mom, I just want to say how incredibly grateful I am for your courage and strength. You did a hell of a job raising Tanasa and me on your own. I don't know how you did it, and I don't know where I'd be without you. I love you."

She looked up and gave me a little smile. "Thank you, Seb. I love you too." I reached over and gave her a hug.

My mom and I laughed and cried, and in the end, we felt closer than we'd been in years. The elephant in the room was finally being addressed. Our conversation opened the door to having more in the future. With each of those talks, I could feel myself slowly becoming whole again.

That was the beginning of my awareness of just how shut down I had been and how isolated I was from my mom and sister prior to that conversation. My survival mechanism since the day my dad died had been to shut out anything related to that loss. I attempted not to feel the bad because it was too overwhelming, but only to feel the good. Because I had been numbing that part of me by running away from the conversation about my father, and ultimately about myself, for so many years, I was never fully myself. All my energy was tied up in hiding my dark side, my shadow. As I began to face my fears and shine some light on the darkness, my relationship and connection with myself, and with others, was deepening immensely.

It was these types of conversations with family and friends that helped me find some of the answers I was looking for. However, they weren't the only means of uncovering information about my dad. In our garage, my mom had kept boxes and boxes of various personal belongings: files, letters, trophies, medals, photographs, and other items which had either belonged to or related to my dad. We moved homes numerous times after he died. One thing that was consistent with the change of scenery was that the boxes always came along with us.

Like the elephant in the room around the stigma of suicide, the boxes in our garage were something I was very aware of, but for the most part avoided. Growing up I had, on occasion, built up the courage to look through some of the boxed items. I never got too far, though. There was something about going through Dad's old things that freaked me out. And, I was terrified of finding out some piece of information that confirmed my belief that I was destined to his same path. Over the years, I learned to avoid those boxes completely. I treated them as if they were haunted or cursed.

I realized after my trip to Australia that those boxes potentially contained a great deal of helpful data for my research. Cursed or not, I made it my mission to slowly and systematically go through all the files and photographs, letters, and bank statements. There was a ton of information right at home that would help me understand the mystery.

Now that I was living in the garage, it was incredibly convenient. I would wait until late at night, after my mom and sister had gone to bed, so I wouldn't be disturbed. I'd choose a box and begin to dig in. Going through the boxes was like going on a roller coaster. Unlike the roller coasters I had avoided growing up, this time I wanted to be on the ride. I wanted to feel the ups and downs and experience it fully. This was very much part of my healing process of learning how to feel again.

The boxes were stacked high along an entire wall of our garage. Some boxes were full of beautiful photographs of my parents from all over the world. These were mostly from the early part of their relationship and around their honeymoon. There were photos of my dad in his youth when he was a Springbok swimming for the South African national team. There were boxes full of swimming medals and trophies, and newspaper and magazine clippings featuring him. It was like looking into a perfect life. All I saw was youth and beauty and winning.

Other boxes had a much different theme. I found files of financial statements, banking, and legal records. Some boxes were full of medical records, giving me further insight into my dad's time in the psychiatric hospital. I even found his death certificate. I found boxes and boxes of letters and cards; letters between my mom and dad in the months before he died and condolence letters my mom had kept from my dad's funeral service. There was a heaviness to the energy around those boxes that was palpable.

In many ways, the boxes were a perfect metaphor for my father. It was like going through the life of two different people, the light and the dark, the winner and the loser, the hero and the failure. Everything seemed so black and white based on the boxes. I remember thinking back on the idea that you're either a winner or a loser. *Maybe it's okay to be both,* I thought.

One night, I came across a postcard from Australia that I hadn't seen before. On the front of the card was a beautiful picture of serene, untouched coastal sand dunes in Western Australia. There was something intriguing, almost haunting, about the photograph. I stared at the picture for a while before turning it over. There I saw the date, May 8, 1990. It was my dad's handwriting and was written just two days before he died. I took a deep breath and slowly continued.

AUSTRALIA

Sand Dunes at Reef Beach between Mt. Barren and Bremer Bay on the south coast of Western Australia.
Photo: Richard Woldendorp No. 129

May 8ᵗʰ 1480

Dearst Sue, Sebastian, Tanessa,

thanks for the cards + letters.
I'm working hard at interviews and I have a couple of promising situations.
I'm missing you all very much.
How I'd love to hold you all and kiss you.
Sebastian it sounds like you're becoming a great boogie boarder
I can't wait to see you in action
Love + hugs + kisses to all
DAD

AIR MAIL

SS+T Slovin
633 Gravilla St
La Jolla
California 92037
United States of America

ART MAIL
AUSTRALIAN IMPRESSIONS

Dearest Sue, Sebastian, Tanasa,

Thanks for the cards and letters. I'm working hard at interviews and I have a couple of promising situations. I'm missing you all very much. How I'd love to hold you all and kiss you. Sebastian, it sounds like you're becoming a great boogie boarder. I can't wait to see you in action.

Love + hugs + kisses to all.

-Dad

I sat there in the garage and slowly ran my fingers across his writing. I read the card over and over. I was reading the words and seeing the love, the hope, and sincerity while knowing what was going on beneath the words. Not written or expressed was the pain, fear, and suffering he was experiencing at the time. I felt both deeply saddened and incredibly touched by his note. I was blown away by the fact that he mentioned me becoming a great boogie-boarder, as my pursuit of that sport had become such a big part of my life.

I turned the card back over and stared at the photograph. Looking at the beautiful blue water, the empty beach and seemingly endless dunes, I thought of my dad's dream of living in such a beautiful and uncrowded place. There was a dreamlike quality to the picture; it gave me a sense of openness, of freedom. Perhaps he chose that particular photograph (consciously or unconsciously) as a symbol of death and the peace and freedom that would come with it. At that moment so much was rising up inside of me. I couldn't help but wonder if he knew he'd be dead by the time we received it.

I kept that postcard in my nightstand and read it often. Among other things, it made me aware of the love my dad had for my mom, sister, and me, an aspect of my relationship with him that I often overlooked. Also, I was doing a great deal of bodyboarding (boogie-boarding) at the time, and I would often think about the note just before competing or going out in big surf. It was another reminder that my dad was with me out in the ocean.

SEBASTIAN SLOVIN

122

CHAPTER 14

THE LAST DAY

I wish I understood the beauty in leaves falling.
To whom are we beautiful as we go?

—David Ignatow

THREE YEARS LATER IN 2006 I HAD THE CHANCE TO GO BACK TO
AUSTRALIA. I was 22 years old at the time. My last visit was when
I had that life-changing conversation with John David, five years
prior. I had learned so much since then. In addition to traveling extensively with my bodyboarding, I'd uncovered a great deal
about my dad's story. While the focus of the trip to Australia was
on bodyboarding, I was looking forward to the opportunity to
continue to learn about my dad.

At the time, the bodyboarding industry was quite small rela-
tive to surfing and other action sports. Many of the world's pro
bodyboarders were on a relatively similar travel schedule, and
because of this, we got to know each other well. It was common
to spend at least part of the (Northern Hemisphere) summer

months in Puerto Escondido, Mexico, and winters on the north shore of Oahu, Hawaii. Many of the best bodyboarders in the world happened to be from Australia. During my travels, I was fortunate to have made some great friends, many of whom were Aussie bodyboarders. My itinerary for this trip was based in part on connecting with my bodyboarder friends across the country.

I spent the first two months of my trip exploring the east coast of Australia, searching for waves and adventure, staying with friends from south of Sydney all the way up north to Cairns. After my time on the east coast, my plan was to head across the country to meet up with my good friend from California, fellow bodyboarder Tyler Weimann. From there we would connect with other Australian bodyboarders and explore the beautiful coast-line and incredible surf around Margaret River. Before heading to Margaret River, however, I had arranged to spend a week with John David and Sara Kennedy in Perth.

One of my regrets from my last trip to Australia was that I didn't have a chance to get together with my dad's cousin Tim. To be honest, it was less that I didn't have the chance and more that I didn't take the chance. One of the main reasons I didn't was that the idea of sitting down with Tim scared the shit out of me. After all, it was at Tim's house where my dad died; he was the one who found my dad's body and made the call to my mom. Also, he had spent the most time with my dad in the days leading up to his death.

Last time around I didn't feel ready to talk to Tim; I didn't think I could handle it. This time, however, my mindset was different. Sitting down and hearing Tim's perspective, if he was open to it, was now something I felt like I could handle and truly wanted to hear.

Before I went to Perth, I spoke with Sara about arranging a time for me to get together with Tim. He and his wife still lived in the neighborhood, so that was convenient. Shortly after I arrived, Sara mentioned that she had made plans for me to see Tim, and I was grateful for his willingness to meet. I had no idea what to expect. I hadn't seen Tim since we were there as a family when I was 5 years old.

Sara shared with me that the suicide was very tough on him and his family, who were all very close to my dad. She also told me that he had been dealing with some health issues of his own and wasn't sure what sort of mental state he was in. I gathered that she was telling me to be prepared for anything.

It was late afternoon when Sara walked me over to Tim's house. While I was grateful for this opportunity, I was also nervous. My heart raced as I approached his front door. After a few knocks and a short wait, Tim welcomed me in with great enthusiasm. He was a very kind man and full of energy, albeit a little scattered. We sat down in his cozy living room and jumped right into catching each other up on life. I updated him on how my family had been doing, and he shared some of the latest from his end. After we had covered the basics, Tim asked if I was interested in taking a little walk along the river before sitting down for dinner. I said that sounded great, and we made our way out.

It was a beautiful evening in Perth; the sun was close to setting and the hot afternoon was transitioning to a pleasantly warm evening. As we made our way down the street, Tim mentioned that this was a walk he took many times before with my father. He then said, rather casually, "Actually, I took this same walk with your dad the night before he died."

Caught off guard by his willingness to jump right into it, I said nothing at first. As we walked, I suddenly felt a strange and familiar sense. At that moment, I couldn't help but put myself in my dad's shoes and wonder what was going through his head that night. It was an eerie experience, to say the least.

I looked over at Tim and asked, "What was he like on that walk? What did you two talk about?"

He replied, "It was a very curious thing, actually, that walk in particular." Tim continued, "As you may know, your father had been staying with us for a few weeks. He was out here doing job interviews and looking for work. Each evening before dinner we would take this same walk around the neighborhood and down by the river, and each evening I could tell that the weight of the world was on his shoulders.

"We would walk and your dad would tell me about how stuck he felt and how he had messed everything up with the mistakes he had made, both personally and financially. I could see it in his eyes, hear it in his voice, even see it in the way he held himself with his head down and shoulders rounded forward. He was in deep. It seemed like he was constantly thinking about and searching for a way out." Tim went on, "The curious thing was that when we were out walking the evening before he died, he was totally different."

I was struck by his last comment. Everything in the background, all the noises and distractions seemed to fade away. I turned to Tim, making brief eye contact as we walked, and asked, "What do you mean he was totally different?"

"Well, he just seemed completely free that evening. He was at peace. We walked through the neighborhood and along the river, and he was saying how beautiful it was here, how clean and fresh the air and how clear the sky. He talked about the clouds and the birds and everything he noticed around him. We had the most pleasant walk, and I remember feeling so relieved and thinking to myself that something had shifted and that Vernon was going to be all right."

"Huh. That's strange," I said, so focused on the conversation that I stopped walking. "I would have thought he would have been a mess at that point, so close to ending it. What do you think that was all about?" I asked.

He stopped and turned to me. "You know, it's something I've thought about a lot since his death. I can't be sure, but I suppose at that point he had already made his decision. He knew he was going to end it in the morning," he said.

I nodded silently, but was still processing what Tim had shared. After some time, I replied, "That makes sense. If the decision had already been made, I suppose he was free at that point."

I looked around at our beautiful surroundings. It was a stunning evening. The sun was now setting. It was beginning to cool off, with a refreshing breeze rolling in. I became aware of the sounds of the birds chirping all around us. The sky was crisp and clear, aside from a few fluffy clouds, with hues of orange and pink slowly floating across the sky. I looked all around us, from the bright sky to the contrast of the dark shades of green in the beautiful trees along the path. I wondered if this was what it was like the evening my dad took his last walk.

We continued to walk slowly down the path in silence. Then, wanting to hear more, I asked Tim what happened after the walk. He shared that they ended up having a wonderful evening. They went back and had dinner with Tim's wife and their two girls, who were teenagers at the time. Vernon was at ease and even laughing for the first time in a long time, Tim recalled. They reminisced about many things, including his competitive swimming days and the trophies he had collected over the years.

We walked along the river until it was nearly dark and then made our way back to Tim's place. While the topic of conversation flowed to different aspects of my dad's life, he remained the central theme of the evening. And as we shared different stories and memories, I found my mind going back to what Tim had shared earlier about my dad's last walk. I couldn't quite put my finger on it, but I knew there was something deeper there, something further to explore.

We eventually made our way back to Tim's place and sat down for a nice dinner. We chatted about all sorts of things that evening. After dinner, we had some tea and the conversation shifted back to the topic of my father, specifically about what happened the morning of Thursday, May 10, 1990, the day of his suicide.

Tim shared with me how he and his wife were preparing for a weekend trip into the bush (which in Australian lingo means wilderness, also called the outback). Everyone was out of the house that morning, and Vernon had a job interview scheduled that day.

Tim's face was tense as he explained how he came home to pick up one last thing for his trip.

"I knew something was up the moment I pulled into the driveway. I could see tire tracks through the grass along the side yard. I got out of my car and followed the tracks around the side of the house until I saw my other car, the one Vernon had been using, in our backyard. My stomach dropped, as I could hear that the engine was still running. As I approached, I could see there was a hose taped to the exhaust pipe which led into the open sliding glass door of our family room. In a panic, I followed the hose into the family room to find Vernon lying dead on the floor with a black trash bag taped over his head, and the other end of the hose was in the trash bag. The place was full of fumes, and I could hardly breathe."

His voice was trembling. Although this was years ago, the memory of the trauma was very much alive.

"I was in shock and didn't know what to do. I pulled the bag off his head to see if it wasn't too late, but he was gone. His face was bloated and pale. I rushed out and turned off the car and then opened all the doors to the house to let it air out. When I came back to his body I noticed a note on the coffee table next to him. The next thing I remember was calling your mom."

Tim continued to share what he remembered of the events that unfolded after that. I sat and listened, hardly breathing and hanging on his every word. After he finished talking, we sat in silence for some time. I had no response.

Tim took a deep breath and continued, "Everyone was absolutely shocked by the news." There was a large and close-knit South African community in Perth, and many knew of Vernon from his swimming days. "Your dad was such a legend, a hero to so many people. How could this have happened to Vernon, of all people? we thought." By more than the words he was sharing I could feel how much my dad meant to him. He then went on to give a brief overview of the days and weeks that followed and how they had a small memorial service for him here in Perth, spreading a portion of his ashes there in the Indian Ocean.

He paused for a moment and looked down, shaking his head from side to side. There was a shift in his energy when he looked back at me, his eyes now intense and piercing.

He said, "To this day I'm still furious with Vernon. How could he have done that at my house! Can you imagine if one of my girls had come home to find him like that?"

His voice was still shaky, but now out of anger rather than fear. As I was listening, I couldn't help but think about past conversations with others about my dad and particularly conversations with my mom. There was a familiar shift from sadness and disbelief to anger and back. It certainly echoed much of my own processing since I began to face my dad's suicide.

I couldn't help but think about the act of suicide, the core of it being not wanting to deal with the anger and frustration and sadness around life. But once that person is gone, where does all that anger and sadness go? Does it just disappear? I wondered if perhaps it gets lodged in those left behind. I could certainly see it in myself, my mom, and many others I spoke with.

While I already knew how my dad had died, the facts I knew were general. Going into the conversation with Tim, I feared hearing the uncensored play-by-play of what had happened. I was worried I wouldn't be able to handle it. To my surprise, it was just the opposite. It was healing for me. Tim didn't hide or sugarcoat anything, which was exactly what I needed.

Getting together with Tim was a monumental part of my journey. It ended up being an amazing experience for me and was incredibly helpful in putting the pieces of the puzzle together. I walked away focused on the catharsis of hearing exactly how the suicide went down. I thought hearing about his death was my main takeaway from visiting Tim. Later, I realized that wasn't the case.

CHAPTER 15

LESSONS FROM A SUICIDE

Truth is one; the sages speak of it by many names.

—The Vedas

I NOW FELT THAT I HAD HOMED IN ON A FEW KEY THEMES AND LESSONS FROM MY QUEST TO LEARN ABOUT MY DAD AND HIS SUICIDE OVER THE PAST FIVE YEARS. Each person I spoke with helped me to piece together the puzzle and gain a better understanding of what happened. On the long flight home from Australia I reflected on my journey and jotted down a few lessons and takeaways that could help guide me moving forward.

Lesson 1: Racing Through Life

One of the most prevalent themes that I heard from nearly every person I spoke with was how goal-oriented my father was. This tied right in with his intensely competitive spirit and his relentless and stubborn quest to be the best in whatever he was doing. Like most people, he set goals relating to many aspects of his life, including his finances, fitness, living situation, etc. Once the goal was set, he would put the blinders on and race toward it. He took what worked for him in competitive swimming and applied those same principles to life. He had been wonderfully successful in the water. In swimming, there is a singular goal in mind, to be first to the finish line, and that is accomplished by charging forward faster than anyone else. In a race, that is a very sound strategy. In life, however, it didn't seem to translate so well.

My dad spent much of his life racing from one goal to the next. He raced forward, putting all his attention on the finish line and missing much of the scenery passing him by. That intense focus on his goals caused him to completely lose touch with the beauty and inherent perfection of what was right there in front of him in the present moment. As a result, life became like a hologram to him, a pale reflection in comparison to the real thing, and he was left feeling empty.

Of course, planning things out and creating goals is useful and necessary. The issue, I came to understand, was how extreme my dad was in his focus on the goal and the future. He was using the present moment as a means for reaching his goal and nothing more. He wasn't happy until he achieved his goal, and whenever he did reach his goal, that happiness or satisfaction was short-lived. He was always on to the next thing.

Lesson 2: Focusing on Money, Image, Status
Another theme of my dad's life that continually came up in the stories I heard was that he placed a great deal of importance on his looks, physical ability, and financial status. My dad was, for

the most part, very successful at what he did. He also happened to be a good-looking guy. From a young age, he was a successful swimmer and took great pride in his physical ability. He found financial prosperity in the business world. For a time, everything was going great; he had his looks, and he was young and wealthy.

Of course, life isn't one straight arrow to the top; there are highs and lows, peaks and valleys. The problem arose when my dad experienced the natural ebb in the cycles of life. When he lost a lot of his money, he reacted to that as if it were a direct blow to his sense of self, which in his mind, it was. As he aged, his looks began to fade and he slowed down physically, and the same thing happened; it was a direct hit to his core identity. It was as if he needed his youth, looks, and money in order to be happy.

The issue wasn't in the material things themselves. Money, good looks, and athletic prestige are wonderful things. The issue was that at his very core, my dad found his sense of self-worth (his personal value) in those extrinsic things, and because of that, he held on to them tightly. In his mind his wealth, societal status, and image made him who he was. Seeing the results of my dad's attachment to and identification with material things and what happened when those things eventually faded or changed was a monumental takeaway for me.

Lesson 3: All or Nothing

Based on the information I had gathered and the stories I heard, it seemed my dad had an all-or-nothing type of mindset. For example, to him, winning was everything. He was only happy when he was winning, which he did most of the time. To him it was black and white: "You're either a winner or a loser." You were either on top of the world or in the gutter. He didn't get the point of doing something unless he was the best.

He certainly instilled this mindset in me when I was young. Later, I began to wonder, *What if there's another way? What if you could play/race for the rush and joy of participating in the activity itself? What if you could let go of the outcome and just be in the moment?* As I explored that in my own life, I experienced the great paradox of competition and performance. I found that I not only enjoyed myself more in sports and academic pursuits when I had a mindful approach, but my results improved as well.

Lesson 4: Fighting with Reality

My father's lack of acceptance was another overarching theme that came up frequently. It manifested in a number of ways, but most noticeably in his vision of a future utopia and fighting with life when things didn't go his way, or resisting the process of getting older. In many ways, his willpower and perseverance served him well: when it came to the determination to win a race, for example. It certainly served as a motivator to get better and to push toward his goals. However, there is a big difference between perseverance and nonacceptance or stubbornness. Perseverance is defined as "continued effort to do or achieve something despite difficulties," and is useful and healthy. On the other hand, lack of acceptance and stubbornness is a resistance to change and doing the same thing repeatedly and expecting different results. My dad spent a great deal of his life and his energy fighting with what is.

ASHES IN THE OCEAN

Toward the end of his life he was in bad financial shape, he wasn't living in the home or location he had dreamed of, many of his relationships were strained, and he was getting older and slowing down physically. Things certainly weren't going according to his plan. Instead of yielding and looking at other options, he put his head down and drove forward, as if he could change his situation through sheer force. As one of his closest friends described it, it was as if he had run right into a brick wall, and instead of lifting his head and looking for a way around, he kept charging forward trying to break through.

Over the course of this journey I came to learn that my dad had some wonderful qualities. He had incredible willpower and determination. He was witty, funny, and charismatic. And at the same time, it became clear that there were many things that did not serve him well. In some ways, he gave me a blueprint for how not to live—and in turn, how to live well from there. He became my greatest teacher.

Vernon (right) at age 8 with his cousin Rob. Cape Town, South Africa. 1953	Vernon at Southern Methodist University (SMU). Dallas, Texas. 1967

VERNON SLOVIN
All-American
200-Yard Butterfly, SWC Champion

Newspaper clipping of Vernon swimming for SMU. Dallas, Texas. 1967

Dad while on vacation with Mom. Mo'orea, French Polynesia. Circa 1979

NEWSFLASH

EX U.C.T. SPRINGBOK ESTABLISHED WORLD SWIMMING RECORD

VERNON SLOVIN, Ikey Springbok swimmer of the mid and late 60's made swimming headlines again in May this year when he broke the world record in the 35-39 year old age-group, for the 200 yds butterfly, at a metting in Los Angeles, California. 35 Year old Slovin, who now resides in La Jolla, near L.A., was timed in at 2 min 00,5 secs. Converted to the 200 metres, he would have clocked in at 2 min 13 sec., which would have won him the silver medal at this year's S.A. National Swimming Championships, held in Port Elizabeth in March. This places his achievement in perspective, and 'Campus Sport' congratulates him, and we are sure all Ikeys do.

It is a pity that Vernon is so far away, as I am sure he must be worth consideration as our Sports Star of the Month.

uct
sports
centre

Mom and Dad's wedding. La Jolla, California. 1981

Vernon breaks Masters swimming world record for men's 200 yd. butterfly. Los Angeles, California. 1980

Vernon out in front at the La Jolla Rough Water Swim.
La Jolla, California. Circa 1981

Off to the races. La Jolla, California. Circa 1981

Postrace. La Jolla, California. Circa 1981

First place at the Rough Water Swim. La Jolla, California. Circa 1981

One of Dad's La Jolla Rough Water Swim gold medals

With Dad on one of my early beach adventures at Windansea.
La Jolla, California. Circa 1984

Bath time. Baja California, Mexico. Circa 1986

Dad and me at grandparents' (Mom's side) house. Los Angeles, California. Circa 1987

Hanging out with Dad postrace. San Diego, California. Circa 1987

In my happy place. La Jolla, California. Circa 1988

Dad and me at Windansea Beach. La Jolla, California. Circa 1988

Dad, sister, and me. Monkey Mia, Australia. 1989

Gearing up for school.
Melbourne, Australia. 1989

Early yoga days with my best bud
John Maher. La Jolla, California. Circa 1990

Mom, Tanasa, and me visiting family. Salt Lake City, Utah. Circa 1994

Fellow bodyboarder Todd Glaser and me at California State Championships.
Huntington Beach, California. 1997

Magazine clipping of me. Puerto Escondido, Mexico. 2004. Photo: Joel Dalmas

Me enjoying the North Shore of Oahu, Hawaii. Circa 2006. Photo: Keith Laub

More bodyboarding from the North Shore of Oahu, Hawaii.
Circa 2006. Photo: Keith Laub

Yoga at Windansea Beach. La Jolla, California. Circa 2010.

-

CHAPTER 16

A DIFFERENT PATH

Breathe! You are alive.

—Thich Nhat Hanh

A FEW YEARS INTO THIS JOURNEY, AS I WAS BEGINNING TO GRASP SOME OF THESE LESSONS, I FOUND MYSELF DRAWN TO THE CONTEMPLATIVE TRADITIONS OF THE WORLD. It started with yoga. I began practicing yoga when I was 16, and my initial motivation was purely for the physical benefits. Yoga was beginning to hit the mainstream in the U.S., and many of my favorite athletes were incorporating yoga into their training regimen, including a lot of the top surfers and bodyboarders. I found yoga to be immensely helpful with all the bodyboarding I was doing. I'd often get tumbled and twisted in crazy ways, especially when the waves were big, and yoga helped me to reduce injuries and stay lean, strong, and flexible. I also found the practice to be restorative after spending long hours in the waves.

For the first several years of doing yoga, I paid very little attention to internal aspects of the practice such as mindfulness and mindset. I enjoyed the physical benefits, and that was enough. As I began to face my dad's suicide and what I had been running away from, I became more drawn to the inner work of yoga and Eastern philosophy in general. Learning about my dad and about yoga was a parallel process in many ways.

By the time I was 20 years old, yoga was up there with body-boarding as two of my favorite activities. Along with my physical practice, I read voraciously on the topics of yoga and Eastern philosophy. I was fascinated with its Hindu origins and many branches. I also practiced meditation along with physical yoga. As my practice and understanding deepened, I became aware of other resources to help guide the way. My study of yoga led me to an interest in Buddhism and Taoism and the practice of mindfulness. From there, I could see the parallels in other contemplative traditions.

The thing I found so mind-blowing about yoga, meditation, and other types of mindful practices and traditions was that they were basically the opposite of how my dad lived and how I had been living. Here were people who had been collectively studying the human condition for thousands of years, and the general teaching was of acceptance and embracing the present moment. All of it was like a breath of fresh air, and I immersed myself in it fully.

During that time, I also began to explore different practices around forgiveness. I came to see that I had been holding on to a lot of anger and resentment toward my dad. Before going to bed at night I would sit and intentionally practice forgiveness toward my dad for the pain and hurt that he had caused my family and me. Some nights I would become full of rage toward him, and other nights I would sit and cry. This practice was incredibly helpful for me in learning how to hold both the anger and the sadness I had in relation to my dad's death. Forgiveness practices, along with yoga and mindfulness meditation, became an outlet for many buried emotions I had been holding on to.

My passion for yoga eventually led me to pursue training to become an instructor. Soon after I received my yoga teacher credential, I began teaching. Becoming a yoga instructor was my way of expressing the life lessons I had learned, and was continuing to learn, about my father.

CHAPTER 17

THE PARADOX

A man will give up almost anything except his suffering.

—John Cleese

OVER THE NEXT FEW YEARS, THINGS REALLY STARTED TO COME TOGETHER FOR ME. My world revolved around my two biggest passions: bodyboarding (and being in the ocean) and yoga. I was doing the things I loved most and getting paid to do them. When I wasn't traveling for bodyboarding or teaching yoga, I was lifeguarding at the beach in Del Mar. Lifeguarding was a natural fit for me. It was also a great way to help stay in shape in between bodyboarding trips while making money at the same time.

I had survived some dark times in my youth and was now on the other side, enjoying life to the fullest. I was in my prime physically and felt wise beyond my years. While in high school, I had been shy and withdrawn, and dating was scarce. Now I was making up for lost time.

During my travels with bodyboarding I not only experienced some of the world's best surf and locations but also hung out with many of the world's top bodyboarders. While the industry was relatively small, the guys on top lived like rock stars. When traveling, I was often included in this inner circle and attempted to live at the same pace as the guys on top. While they certainly trained hard and put a great deal of focus on their craft, they also partied and chased women at a level I hadn't seen before. It wasn't long before I was fitting in quite well.

One winter in Hawaii, one of my sponsors rented a house for the team riders to stay in during the winter season. The house was on the beach on the North Shore of Oahu, just a short walk from the infamous Pipeline and a handful of other world-class surf spots. Each year, it was common for pro bodyboarders to spend the month of January (and often longer) on the North Shore, which is the mecca of surfing and bodyboarding. It was a four-bedroom house and there were at least 12 of us staying there, ranging in age from 16 to 30. The team riders hailed from a variety of places, including the East and West Coasts of the U.S., Australia, South Africa, and France.

The Aussies were by far the craziest of the bunch, both in and out of the water. They seemed to have no fear. No matter how crazy the surf got, they were not only up for it but amped. They were amped to surf, to drink and party, and to get girls. Regardless of age or origin, there was a ton of competition among our team to get the best photos and video footage out in the water, and we certainly put in our time in that respect. There was also a lot of competition (maybe more) around who could get the most girls. Within a couple of days one of the Aussies created a formal contest around who could get the most action and how far they could go. It was known as the hookup chart, a large piece of construction paper taped to the living room wall with each of our names on it and a graph tracking the number of hookups and how far we went.

I made it my purpose to not only be the best out in the water but to win the hookup chart. After four weeks of surfing, lots of drinking, and lots of women, I came out on top. It was a close race, but I edged out a young Aussie for the win. These types of shenanigans happened not only in Hawaii, but all over.

When I wasn't bodyboarding I would practice, teach, and fully immerse myself in yoga. Along with being a top bodyboarder, I had my sights set on being a world-class yoga instructor. After a few years of teaching, I was off to a good start. I taught at a popular yoga studio, had developed a strong following, and was making a name for myself in the industry. It also didn't hurt that I was young, fit, and good looking, and that most of my clients were women.

People enjoyed my classes and I enjoyed teaching. I loved expressing to my students the importance of being in the moment. These were concepts that I knew very well from the lessons I had learned from my dad. They were alive in me. I didn't feel like I was just repeating from some ancient text that I had read.

With this *knowing* came a sense that I had it all figured out. While I certainly had learned some very valuable lessons from my dad, I had, without realizing it, gone off the tracks a bit. My intention to be a world-class yoga teacher had originally come from wanting to help others, but along the way the focus had shifted to be all about me. I was beginning to take my yoga practice and myself far too seriously. I was becoming more interested in how awesome I looked and how advanced I was than in the quality of my teaching or my presence. Yoga had become a way for me to inflate my rapidly growing ego. I used it and the spiritual-sounding language to charm women and get what I wanted.

All cylinders were firing; I was traveling, bodyboarding, practicing and teaching yoga, partying, and chasing women. And while all this was happening I felt confused, because no matter what I did, beneath the surface I rarely felt satisfied, at least not for long. At first this was so subtle I hardly recognized it. As time went on, however, this general sense of dissatisfaction grew from a whisper to an undeniable presence.

I felt like I had it all figured out. I had everything I thought I wanted, but at the same time, there seemed to be something missing. With bodyboarding, I found myself becoming frustrated and angry if things didn't go my way. If I didn't perform my best in a competition or if the waves weren't good enough, I would easily become distraught. It got to the point where I found myself excited to bodyboard only when there was someone photographing or taking video of me. What had started out as pure passion and a wonderful physical and creative outlet now felt mechanical and empty. If I had a photographer or videographer with me, I was completely focused on getting the perfect shot or video clip as opposed to enjoying my time out in the ocean and doing what I loved.

I had the incredible opportunity to visit some of the world's most beautiful places and bodyboard some of the best waves. Yet, when the waves went flat or the conditions got bad, I found myself wishing I was somewhere else. I would be in Mexico, wishing I was in Australia, or in Hawaii and wishing I was in Tahiti.

When it came to relationships, it was a similar story. Even when I thought I was with the right person, my sense of satisfaction was short-lived. I dated some amazing people, but it wasn't long before I was off looking for the next one. From age 18 to 25 I went through women at an alarming rate.

In my yoga practice and teaching, what I thought was mindfulness had turned more into self-centeredness. It was all about me: how advanced *my* practice was, how spiritual *I* was, how awesome *I* was. I had unknowingly become very attached to the idea of being a world-class yoga teacher and more specifically to the perks that I imagined came with it. I thought I knew it all and had a very clear vision of my future.

CHAPTER 18

THE FINAL TRIP

Nothing is as invisible as the obvious.

—Richard Farson

By my midtwenties I had settled down a bit. I'd been dating my girlfriend at the time, Lisa, for over a year. I was doing well teaching yoga and still traveling regularly for bodyboarding. However, I continued to feel like there was something missing. I believed that I was feeling unfulfilled because I didn't have closure in my journey of learning about my father and his suicide. I needed a way to feel complete so I could properly move forward with the next chapter of my life.

It was around this time that an opportunity for closure presented itself. My mom told me that she had been holding on to the remains of my dad's ashes in a tin box that she had kept in her closet. We decided to divide the remaining ashes between Tanasa and me. The idea was that we could each do what we wished with his remains. As soon as we discussed this, I had a vision of spreading his ashes in the ocean off Cape Town. In my mind, taking his remains back to South Africa, his homeland, was a fitting ending to his journey and to mine.

I wasted no time in beginning to plan this trip to South Africa and what I saw as the final step of my quest. By this point I had traveled extensively through my bodyboarding career, but hadn't yet been to South Africa (I had been with my parents as a baby, but had no recollection of my time there). My plan was to spend six weeks in South Africa to visit my extended family, explore the country, and of course, spread my father's ashes. Lisa would fly out and join me for a portion of the trip, as she was in school and couldn't take that much time away.

Growing up, I had heard so much about South Africa from my dad and family friends that I had developed a strong tie to the place. My dad had told me all sorts of crazy stories from his upbringing there: shark sightings while swimming in the waters off Cape Town, riding ostriches, and being chased by rhinos out in the bush. I was very much looking forward to having some context and experience of the places I had heard so much about.

I had arranged to stay with my dad's cousin, Rob Spence, and his family in Cape Town. Rob and his wife Noreen had two sons, Richard and David, who were both a few years older than I was. I had been in touch with Rob off and on via email over the past few years. He had been incredibly helpful to me in learning about my dad's early years and upbringing. He and my dad had attended the same schools from when they were four years old all the way through secondary school.

As the trip got closer I found myself putting a great deal of focus on the significance of spreading my dad's ashes. In my mind, this was sure to give me closure, and it would be the storybook ending to my journey of learning the lessons from my father and his suicide. Before going to bed at night I would visualize this final act, and I imagined the wave of understanding and enlightenment that was sure to follow.

When I arrived in Cape Town with my dad's ashes in tow, after the long trip from Los Angeles (via Paris and Johannesburg), Rob was there to pick me up from the airport. He was a strong and stocky man with a sun-weathered face and a heart of gold. I learned right away that he was a man of few words while being incredibly witty when he spoke. I liked him immediately.

It was midafternoon when I arrived, and before going home, Rob was eager to give me a brief tour of the city. As we drove into the city I was blown away by the natural beauty of the land. I had seen photos and heard many people describe the scenery, but none of that did it justice. The physical beauty of Cape Town was unparalleled. No city I'd seen could compare to it.

From the airport, we drove through the city center to an affluent coastal community called Sea Point. Rob shared that this was where my dad and his brother Brian grew up. We stopped along the side of the road and he pointed out the exact condo where they had lived, although it had been remodeled since. I was amazed by the similarities between Sea Point and La Jolla; there was an uncanny resemblance and feel. I was mesmerized by the stunning views as we continued to drive along the coast. The contrast between the deep blue water and the dark gray rocks and cliffs of the coastline was spectacular.

And to see Table Mountain towering in the background only made it more impressive.

We parked in a small and somewhat crowded parking lot. Rob turned the car off, looked at me, and said with a smile, "This was your dad's very favorite place, Clifton 4th Beach. Let's have a look, shall we?"

I followed him through the parking lot to a lookout point near a staircase which led down to the beach. I stopped above the stairs and looked out. The crystal-clear aquamarine water was spectacular against the bright white sand. A few dozen people with their bright towels and umbrellas dotted the cove, which was surrounded on both sides by a rocky outcropping of large, smooth granite boulders. It was one of the most beautiful beaches I had ever seen.

We walked down the steps to the sand. At the bottom of the staircase was the lifeguard station. I paused to watch a couple of lifeguards sitting on the deck looking out over the swimmers. I imagined my dad having been there as a teenager. I wondered what he would have been like in his youth. I stood for a moment next to Rob and took in the scenery. While it was fairly crowded, the U shape of the beach and the rocks on either side gave it a secluded feel. Several yachts were docked out in the deeper water. There was hardly any wind, and the calm water sparkled in the afternoon sun. Most of the beachgoers were lying out on the sand enjoying the sun, and some were in the shallows playing in the small waves.

I rolled up my pants and strolled down to the water's edge. The sand was hot from the afternoon sun. When I got down to the water, a small wave rushed up over my feet. I gasped in shock as the water felt like ice, especially in contrast to the heat of the day. I stood with my feet tingling in the chilly water and looked at the beauty all around me. I knew this was the place to spread my dad's ashes.

We made our way to Robert's home, which was about a 20-minute drive through the city center and around the back side of Table Mountain. When we arrived, the Spence family welcomed me with open arms. Although I hadn't seen them since I was a little tyke, we had a bond that seemed to go back generations. I connected with Richard and David right away. That first evening we were all hanging out and exchanging stories after dinner. Rob got up from the table and came back with several old photo albums. As I turned the pages I was blown away to see pictures of Rob and my dad and my uncle Brian as young boys mixing it up on the beach and around the countryside. Rob sat beside me and occasionally chimed in with a story or context to add to the photos.

I spent that first week exploring Cape Town and the surrounding area. The Spences were wonderfully gracious hosts, guiding me all around the city, visiting the main attractions along with my dad's favorite places and hangouts. It was incredible to see the community and landscape where my dad grew up. We visited Long Street Baths, the pool where he first trained and raced as a 10-year-old. We drove out to the ranchland where my dad spent time with his family away from the city, passing his days playing sports, riding horses, and exploring the outdoors. Visiting all these places was like visiting the most holy of temples; I walked around in awe of their beauty and could feel the presence of my dad.

Lisa arrived one week into the trip, and after spending a few more days in Cape Town, we set out to explore more of the country. We flew to a small town called Nelspruit in the northeastern part of the country. From there we rented a car and spent a few days adventuring around Kruger National Park observing lions, elephants, giraffes, and other incredible animals I had only seen previously in zoos. After Kruger, we traveled south through Swaziland, and then to Durban, the Wild Coast, Port Elizabeth, and the Garden Route. My extended family on my dad's side were spread out all over the country and we were able to stay with several of them over the course of our travels. At each stop I learned more about my dad and the land he grew up in. It was an amazing adventure, and we even had the opportunity to go shark-cage diving! Sufficiently exhausted and satisfied from our journey, we eventually made it back to Cape Town.

After a few more days in Cape Town, it was time for Lisa to head back to San Diego and back to school. I was scheduled to stay in Cape Town for one more week before returning home. I spent most of my time with David and Richard hanging out and enjoying Clifton's 4th Beach.

CHAPTER 19

ASHES
IN THE
OCEAN

The river is everywhere.

—Hermann Hesse

O<small>N MY LAST DAY IN</small> C<small>APE</small> T<small>OWN</small> I <small>HAD ARRANGED TO FINALLY</small> <small>SPREAD MY DAD'S ASHES</small>. It was a spectacular day as I stared out at the shimmering blue Atlantic Ocean. With Rob by my side, we stood at the top of the stairs leading down to Clifton 4th Beach. In my right hand, I held a bag that contained a copper tin with the remains of my dad. I closed my eyes and felt the sun on my face as I reflected on the journey of his ashes. Some of them had been spread in the Indian Ocean where he died in Perth, Australia, and some in the Pacific at the La Jolla Cove. It was only fitting to bring his final remains back to Cape Town, the place where he started his journey.

I reflected on the adventure and fun over the past six weeks, and the memories flashed through my mind. I had reconnected with the land and with the extended family I had heard so much about but barely knew. Those memories faded into the background as I refocused on the task before me and the honor of spreading the remainder of my dad's ashes. Rob and I walked in silence down the long staircase to the cove. Rob stayed on the high sand of the beach near the lifeguard tower as I slowly made my way past the crowds on the beach. I felt the warm sand beneath my feet with each step. I reached the far end of the cove and walked around an outcropping of dark gray rocks to a secluded part of the beach. My feet tingled in the cold as I walked through the clear shallow water.

I found a place between the rocks and away from the crowd that was perfect. I took out the box and opened it, looking down at the ashes. I thought about my dad's path in life, starting here in this town at this beach and then traveling to live in the United States. I thought about all his adventures around the world, living it up, and then his death in Australia. I imagined all the different beaches my dad must have visited and all the different oceans he swam in. Then I took a moment to reflect on his influence on my path. I recalled all the traveling I had done, all the oceans I had swum and surfed in. I contemplated the journey I had been on to put the pieces of my father's life back together so I could understand it and learn from it. I thought about everything leading up to this point and how in my mind this was the perfect ending to my father's journey, a complete circle back to his home, the beautiful ocean in South Africa.

I waded out into the chilly water, took a deep breath, and turned the box over to set my dad's ashes free. I watched as the ashes fell into the clear water, some of them sinking below and some floating on the surface. A little wave came and mixed them up further. In a few moments, they were gone. Just like that.

I walked back around the rocks through the cold shallow water. I made my way across the warm sand on the beach, casually tossing the tin box into a rubbish bin as I passed. I dusted off my hands as if to say I was done; I had completed my mission. I found Rob waiting for me near the bottom of the stairs by the lifeguard station.

We didn't talk much on the drive back home, I just looked out the window at the incredible scenery and smiled. I felt a deep sense of gratitude for having the opportunity to complete my journey. I was now ready to move forward with the next chapter of my life.

CHAPTER 20

OFF TRACK

Born of a broken man. Never a broken man.

—Zack de la Rocha

I RETURNED TO SAN DIEGO FEELING COMPLETE AND READY TO MOVE ON TO THE NEXT CHAPTER OF MY LIFE. I chose to focus on yoga and on becoming a world-class instructor. I continued to bodyboard and lifeguard, while focusing the majority of my attention on developing my yoga skills. I stepped up my efforts and enrolled in additional teacher trainings. With my personal yoga practice, I put in more time on the mat and pushed my body to do more advanced postures.

It was around this time that I began to experience an intense pain in my left hip. I had experienced occasional hip pain in the past, but this was different. This pain was severe and persistent. I couldn't figure it out. I was in great shape overall, practicing yoga, bodyboarding, and exercising every day. I wondered, *How could I have hip pain at my age?* The pain was most acute when I was in certain positions while doing yoga, surfing, and bodyboarding. Basically, it hurt most during the activities I loved. Which, coincidentally, also happened to be the activities I felt the most defined by and successful in.

I didn't change my routine much at first. I tried to push through it and figured the pain would go away. It only got worse. It got to the point where my own yoga practice was severely limited, and my hip was affecting my teaching because I had trouble demonstrating even simple poses. As the pain grew more intense, I even had to take a break from surfing and bodyboarding. This wasn't the start to the new chapter of life I had envisioned.

I had experienced a variety of different injuries throughout my bodyboarding career, from concussions and lacerations to ligament and muscle tears. So, I was familiar with what it took to heal and get back to business. While I was no stranger to injury, I had always struggled with taking time off from the activities I loved. This was no exception. As my movement became more limited, my anxiety grew. When it became apparent that this wasn't just going to go away with a little rest, I began a frantic search to find help to get back to doing the things that I loved. I went to physical therapists, massage therapists, doctors, acupuncturists, energy workers, and postural therapists. My diagnosis was all over the map, from hip flexor tendonitis, to low back weakness, to an inability to express myself creatively (depending on who you asked).

Over the next few months, I saw dozens of specialists and tried a wide variety of healing practices and methods. I ended up at my last resort, an orthopedic surgeon, getting an MRI with ultrasound. The surgeon found that I had a labral tear, along with a small piece of bone that was floating around in my left hip socket that he mentioned was probably from some past trauma.

I'd had several particularly bad bodyboarding wipeouts over the past few years, and I thought back on one that was the most likely culprit. On my last trip to Australia I was at a surf spot called the Box, which is near Margaret River in Western Australia. The Box is notoriously dangerous and is known for intensely powerful waves which break over a very shallow reef. On my last wave, I didn't quite make it out of the barrel, and as I got pulled under, my left shin and knee slammed onto the reef. I was then tumbled around violently several times before making it back to the surface. I came up in a panic, as I thought I had broken my leg. After a long and painful paddle in, I hobbled up onto the beach and looked down to see a cut in my wetsuit and blood pouring down my shin. Fortunately, there was no break, but my left hip was sore for days as it felt like my leg got jammed into my pelvis.

Now that this hip pain was persistent, the recommended treatment according to the surgeon was to go under the knife, which was not a path I wanted to go down. I was terrified by the thought that I'd have surgery and come out being worse off than before. Or, that I wouldn't be able to get back to doing yoga and surfing at the level I had been. I couldn't go through with it. So, I went back to the drawing board. I was going to fix this thing nonsurgically; after all, I was a yoga instructor, for crying out loud! I couldn't be having hip surgery, especially at my age. I went back to seeing a variety of therapists, got more acupuncture treatments, and did countless posture and strengthening exercises, but nothing worked.

Several months later, with no major change in my hip pain status, I decided to bite the bullet and go through with hip surgery. The plan was for the surgeon to repair the tear in my hip socket and clean out any debris while he was in there. I just wanted to be done with this and get back to doing what I felt like I was born to do. Fortunately, the surgery went well and there were no complications. My mom was kind enough to offer to take care of me during my recovery and rehabilitation process. She set up an inflatable bed in the downstairs living room of her house so I wouldn't have to deal with the stairs.

Being laid up in bed was difficult for me, to say the least. I was used to doing my daily yoga practice plus a ton of other physical activity every day, and going from that to just lying on my back was torture. I struggled the first few days after the surgery. I felt agitated and anxious; I couldn't help but feel like this shouldn't be happening, that I should never have had to get surgery in the first place. This was not the path I had planned on taking. My vision was to become a world-renowned yoga instructor, and this was a direct threat to my dream. It was still too early to tell if the surgery had taken care of my hip pain, but I kept anxiously wondering what I'd do if I couldn't make a full comeback. Or, what would I do if I still had pain even after the surgery?

I tried my hardest to embrace the downtime and the stillness, but it wasn't happening. I was scheduled to begin physical therapy in three weeks and was counting down the days until I was finally allowed to get back to moving again; I couldn't wait. The days leading up to physical therapy seemed like some of the longest of my life. I struggled with having to stay in bed, with the loss of my independence, and with maintaining a positive outlook. I worried and ruminated over my future and the uncertainty around my physical ability moving forward.

When the day of my physical therapy appointment eventually came, I was elated. Finally, I had something to help me move forward. The appointment went well, and at the end I was given a few rudimentary exercises to gently strengthen the muscles around my left hip. I assured the therapist that I was a high-level athlete and that he could pile on the exercises. He just smiled and reassured me that this would get me to where I wanted to go. Before I left he said, "Sebastian, remember to be patient and take it slow. There is a lot of healing left to be done, and this isn't a race." I smiled and nodded in understanding as I hobbled out of his office on crutches.

To say that I ignored his words of advice would be an understatement. That afternoon I completed the exercises he gave me for homework and then some. I got a little carried away and threw a few of my own physical therapy moves into the mix. I was going to fast-track this thing to recovery. The next morning, I got up and was at it again. This time I took my moves a little too far and felt a twinge of sharp pain. I didn't think much of it initially, but later when I went to take a shower, I found an unusual and painful bulge on my hip directly under one of the scars I had from surgery. *What the hell is this?* I wondered. To my dismay, the painful lump didn't go away, but got worse as I moved throughout the day.

I soon found myself back with the orthopedic surgeon to check it out. Being in that office again was the last place I wanted to be. After disrobing, I spent 30 minutes in my medical gown anxiously waiting for the surgeon. When he finally arrived, I made my way from the chair to the examination table.

"I'm not sure what happened. All of a sudden this lump just appeared," I explained, trying to appear as if I wasn't the cause of this mishap. I grimaced in pain as the surgeon probed my mysterious hip bump. He had a curious look on his face as he silently examined my hip. Then in a surprised and almost amused tone he said, "In all my years of doing this surgery, I've never seen anything like this before." He went on to tell me that it looked like a muscle had herniated out of one of the incision points from surgery that they had stitched up. Apparently, I had indeed overdone it in PT.

"Not to worry," the doc assured me, "we can get this taken care of. We just need to get you back in for surgery." After realizing that he wasn't joking around, my mental state went from bad to worse. *How could this be happening? This wasn't part of my yoga/wellness/healer master plan at all. WTF!*

My second round of surgery was scheduled for one week later. It was the earliest they could get me in. When I finally got home that afternoon after sitting in traffic for an hour, I was a defeated man. I didn't know what to do. I couldn't believe this was happening. Now my physical therapy for the original surgery would be postponed a month due to this second surgery, and there was a myriad of possible complications that went along with that. Over that amount of time, the scar tissue buildup from the original surgery could be a threat to getting my range of motion back. If that were the case, I might even have to go in for a third surgery to remove the scar tissue from the first surgery. My mind was spinning from all the terrifying possibilities. Logically I knew that compared to what many people go through in terms of physical limitation, this was small potatoes. To me, though, it felt like I had a life-threatening illness.

Back home I slowly crutched my way through the living room and sat on the somewhat deflated inflatable bed and sulked. I ran my fingers over the painful lump on my hip, and in feeling the pain, grew angrier at my hip. *How could my body have let me down like this?* My thoughts began to spiral out of control. *What am I going to do for money?* I panicked. All my avenues for making money were physical. A fact that I was now acutely aware of. This was my version of a stock market collapse. Not only was this a financial crisis, but more importantly, who would I be without my physical ability? I wouldn't be a master yoga instructor. No respectable woman would want to be with me. I would end up homeless and alone with a bad hip. *What was the point of going on if I couldn't move like I once could?*

I spent the next several days wallowing in the darkness. I was frustrated and fed up. I felt a deep surge of anger rising with a quality and intensity I hadn't felt in a long time. Somehow, I had regressed to the familiar but distant darkness of my adolescence. I was angry that I had to go back into surgery, I was angry at my hip and body for not cooperating, and for the first time in years, I found myself blaming my dad for the situation I was in.

CHAPTER 21

DIE BEFORE YOU DIE

Who would you be without your story?

—Byron Katie

EVERYTHING CAME TO A HEAD THE NIGHT BEFORE MY SECOND SURGERY. I had hardly slept all week, and this night was no different. I was tossing and turning, worrying about how surgery was going to go and frustrated that I was even in this position to begin with. It felt like my head was going to explode from everything swirling around inside.

I also found myself thinking over and over again about my dad and why he'd done what he'd done. I replayed some of the conversations I'd had about him over the past several years. Instead of remembering the helpful lessons, on this night I was finding reasons to justify my anger. I remember hearing my mom say, "One of the things that saddened me the most was that when your dad died, that was the end of your childhood." Every thought seemed to tie back to blaming my dad in one way or another. I firmly believed that if he hadn't died by suicide, I wouldn't be in this situation today. I was back playing a role I knew all too well; I was the victim and my dad and life were the perpetrators.

As I was lying in bed with these thoughts churning around, I suddenly felt an eerie sensation, a deep and powerful resonance with my dad, similar to déjà vu. I felt like I was in his shoes toward the end of his life. It was the feeling of being trapped, with no way out. I stared up at the ceiling and looked around at the dark and lonely room. *How could this have happened to me?* Everything I had learned over the course of this journey, and all I had been doing—yoga, mindfulness, and meditation, etc.—had been to avoid finding myself in this exact situation. I certainly didn't have it all figured out. In fact, maybe I had it all wrong.

I then thought back on one person and conversation in particular. I recalled the evening walk I took with my dad's cousin Tim when I was in Perth. I thought about what Tim had said that evening, how he described my dad having made such a dramatic shift the day before his suicide. How he went from feeling totally trapped and deeply depressed one day to free, at peace, and clear the next. Of course, that was once he made the decision to end his life.

I closed my eyes and suddenly I had a vision. It was like I was dreaming, but I was awake. I was in my dad's body walking next to Tim during that final evening. I looked around the beautiful surroundings: the green grass and tall trees along the bank of the river, the water slowly flowing downstream, the fluffy clouds slowly floating by in shades of orange and pink from the setting sun. I could hear the birds chirping all around us. I could see Tim's face as we walked. I could see it all. I was my dad. I (he) felt completely free and at peace in that moment.

I opened my eyes, and there I was back in my dark room. It was the middle of the night, but a hint of light came in through the blinds from the street lights outside. I thought back to my dad and everything that was going on in his life at the time of that walk. His marriage was strained, he was facing financial ruin, and he had the pressure of supporting two young children. He was struggling with getting older and slowing down physically, and his looks were fading. He was no longer the superstar he once was. His thoughts of regret and failure drained him to the point where he could no longer see or appreciate what he did have. In addition to his loving wife and two healthy children, he had an education that would allow him to pursue many different career paths. As far as material wealth was concerned, he had far more than most people on this planet.

His thoughts about his situation eventually made him sick with depression and anxiety. All that built up to the point where suicide felt like his only option. While he was undoubtedly in a difficult situation, his shift and freedom the day before he died showed me that the primary cause of his unhappiness and suffering was his thoughts about his situation, **not the situation itself.**

I wondered, *What if he had been able to make that shift and continued to go on living?* In other words, what if he had been able to make the choice to completely accept his life situation and circumstances, and not kill himself the next day? Maybe he wouldn't go on to fulfill his dream of owning a big house in the perfect location. Or, maybe he would. Who knows? Perhaps he'd go on to be a tomato farmer, or a swim coach, or maybe he wouldn't work at all.

What a curious thing that he could be totally overwhelmed and depressed one day, and after changing his perspective (through seeing a way out), he could then be free. Nothing about my dad's life situation had actually changed during the time between when he made the decision to kill himself and the act of doing it. All that had happened was a shift in his perspective, and suddenly his whole world was changed. What a crazy realization!

It hit me like a bolt of lightning. How do I make that same shift in perspective *and,* most importantly, go on living?

After all the time and energy I had spent learning from my dad and his suicide, was I really saying I couldn't go on without my physical ability? Here I was doing the very things my dad had done; I had adopted the same mindset that caused him so much suffering and strife. In a sneaky, ninja-like way, my sense of self-worth had become completely tied up in my physical ability. *How could this have happened? How could I not have seen it coming?* I was racing toward my perceived finish line—recovering from my hip injury so I could get back on my path to becoming an amazing yoga instructor—as fast as I possibly could. I was fighting with reality and paying very little attention to what my body actually needed.

There is a concept in Buddhist philosophy called "Die before you die." I later came to learn this notion exists in many different spiritual and religious traditions. To die before you die is a metaphorical killing of your past self. It is letting go of the attachments to the thoughts, stories, and beliefs that had defined you.

I understood now that this was what my dad did. Of course, my dad didn't do this intentionally. The key, I realized, was for me to do what my dad did, as in let go of my story and metaphorically die to the past, and then go on living. It was now clear to me that once you "die before you die," then you can truly go on living.

There I was in bed, with a crazy lump on my hip, the night before a second hip surgery. I had no idea how long it would be until I was back to surfing and yoga and all that. I ran my hand over the lump on my hip. It was still sore to touch, but strangely it didn't hurt. It was an odd sensation. I could feel the physical pain, but there was something completely different about it; the emotional pain that I had added to the injury was gone. I realized that all the stories and thoughts I had about my situation—*I'm ruined without a fully functioning hip, no one will respect me without my physical ability, I won't be able to support myself, no one will love me, etc.*—were so much worse than the actual physical discomfort I had been dealing with. I felt immense gratitude toward my dad for teaching me this valuable lesson.

I also was in touch with something deeper. Prior to this, I felt like I had an intellectual understanding of the lessons I had learned from my dad's life and death. Now I was beginning to have a more embodied knowing of those lessons. I was also able to see that my dad really did the very best he could, given the circumstances he was facing and his level of understanding at the time. In that moment of understanding I was able to wholly forgive my father.

The tension in my body melted away. I just lay there in bed and couldn't help but smile. I felt a shift in my energy. There was no more resistance. A deep sense of peace settled over me. To be clear, nothing had changed aside from my perspective. Nothing had changed, yet everything had changed. That realization marked the beginning of my actual rehabilitation, the first step of my hip healing. I drifted off into a deep and peaceful sleep.

CHAPTER 22

A PERFECT CIRCLE

You need not leave your room. Remain sitting at your table and listen. You need not even listen, simply wait. You need not even wait, just learn to become quiet, and still, and solitary. The world will freely offer itself to you unmasked. It has no choice; it will roll in ecstasy at your feet.

—Franz Kafka

I AWOKE THE NEXT MORNING FEELING RESTED AND AT EASE. I went in for my second surgery with no resistance. The surgery and process of recovery afterward was completely different without the emotional pain I had previously attached to it. There was still physical discomfort, but it was free from the inner turmoil I had experienced the first time around. During my recovery, I would sit next to a window or by an open door for hours and simply observe life as it unfolded around me. The world had taken on a new depth and richness that, for the most part, had been hidden from me before.

My favorite pastime was to watch the hummingbirds that would frequent the plants and flowers outside my front door. I'd sit back and watch as they'd dart in and hover in front of the flowers, taking in little sips of nectar. Occasionally, two or more would show up at the same time and I'd watch amused as they chased each other around.

Since I was young I had developed a strong connection to hummingbirds. From what I observed, they lived extraordinary lives, zooming from flower to flower, chasing mates, and sometimes getting into little scuffles with other birds in their territory. The fights never seemed too serious, though, and would be over in moments. To me they represented a sense of lightness and freedom and joy. I imagined my dad reincarnated as a little hummingbird zooming around looking for food and mates with few cares beyond that.

Once I became a little more mobile, I often visited a nearby park. One morning when I got to the park, there was not a soul around. There was a chill in the air and it was quite blustery. The ground was slick from the morning showers, but the rain had stopped for the time being. Leaves swirled around me as I slowly crutched my way past the duck pond and found a spot to sit near my favorite willow tree. I laid down my blanket and rested, taking in the fresh air and watching as the clouds gathered and moved across the sky.

I thought back to a cherished pastime as a boy, flying kites at the park with my dad. He would set everything up for me, and then once it was ready, I'd take the spool of string and run. "Faster,

faster," he'd yell as I ran barefoot across the grass. After we got the kite up in the air, if there was enough wind, we would lie back on the grass and watch the kite and the clouds floating above. I wondered what it would be like to be back with my dad again.

I was pulled out of my daydream as tiny drops of rain began to fall from the sky. I gazed up as the clouds began to darken overhead. I closed my eyes and took a few deep breaths, enjoying the feeling of the raindrops falling on me. As the rain began to fall harder, I scooted closer to the trunk of the willow tree to get some cover from the downpour. I was mostly protected from the rain, besides the occasional drop through the leaves here and there. I stared out across the park as the rain fell; no one else was around. I then looked down at my rain-soaked clothes and the tiny drops of water on the back of my hands.

Suddenly I heard a powerful buzzing noise. I looked up to see a hummingbird hovering right in front of me! I froze, startled initially, and then mesmerized as the tiny bird seemed to be staring directly at me. I could feel the buzzing in my chest and throughout my body. The bird was still, yet intense at the same time. It hovered just a couple of feet in front of me for what seemed like ages. Then it suddenly belted out a little hummingbird call and flashed the ruby red feathers around its throat before it zoomed off over the trees and into the distance. It seemed like the hummingbird was trying to tell me something.

I sat there and looked around with a smile, in awe of what had just happened. I gazed down again at the tiny drops of water on the back of my hands and shivered a bit as a cold breeze blew by. I thought back to learning about the water cycle when I was in grade school: how the sun shines down and heats up the water from the oceans, rivers, and lakes, which then evaporates into the air, forming clouds, and then the clouds bring water back to the land through fog, rain, hail, sleet, or snow in a process that is continually moving without any beginning or end.

And then I thought back to moments earlier when I wondered what it would be like to be with my dad again. Looking down at the drops of water on my hands, I realized that he was, in fact, right here with me. He was in much more than the ocean. He was all around me, in everything! He was there, not only in the raindrops, but in the grass and trees, in all the plants and all the animals. It occurred to me that I had been viewing the world from a very limited perspective. I thought about how silly it was to only feel that connection, that oneness with life, in one setting, which for me had been in the ocean. *What about the rest of my life?* I thought. I had been missing the point!

I had traveled all over the world searching out different people and places, looking to uncover some life secret or grand realization that would, in the end, leave me feeling complete, whole, enlightened. *What an absurd idea!* I thought. *How could I ever be separate from my dad or he be separate from me? For that matter, how can anyone or anything be separate from anything else?* I had been whole all along, only I hadn't realized it. I sat under the willow tree, soaking wet, and looked around in wonder at the incredible scenery, feeling gratitude and a deep knowing that I was one with everything around me. I felt nothing but lightness and love for my father, for life, and for this ongoing journey.

Illustration by Blaze Syka

EPILOGUE

AFTER SURGERY, I SLOWLY BUT SURELY MADE MY WAY BACK TO YOGA, SURFING, AND THE PHYSICAL ACTIVITIES I LOVED. My hip injury and the process of recovery turned out to be a wonderful teacher. Prior to surgery I had taken so much of my physical ability for granted. During my recovery process, even going on a short walk under my own power was a gift.

I experienced a shift in the way I approached physical activities. Over the years my ability in surfing and bodyboarding had become so enmeshed with my sense of self-worth. My surgery and recovery was like hitting a reset button. It was an opportunity to start anew, to see that my physical ability did not dictate my sense of self-worth. I returned to surfing and bodyboarding motivated by what's inside me—my love and enthusiasm for the sport—rather than doing them to impress or prove myself to others, or out of the fear of what I'd lose if I didn't do them. The process has been one of returning to a childlike wonder and joy.

I'm still very much interested in progressing and honing my skills, only now there is a renewed sense of freedom, fun, and creativity. I've had a similar experience with my yoga practice. Before surgery, my personal value was connected to my ability to do advanced postures and my focus was on looking the part of a master yogi. Post-surgery, my practice has been about honoring my body and doing exactly what I am able to do. Like surfing, I still pursue new knowledge and continue to develop my practice and do so with a different mindset.

I also experienced a shift and deepening in my relationship with nature. Initially inspired by my father, my connection with nature is one that I continue to cultivate daily. In addition to it being a great teacher, there is something about nature that encourages a sense of wonder in the world and intimacy with the unknown. Whether going for a swim in the ocean or a walk in the park, spending time unplugged from technology and out in nature has become a central part of my personal practice for self-care and well-being.

LESSONS REVISITED

As I write this, it has been 27 years since my father's suicide. I feel incredibly fortunate to be on this path and thankful for the lessons I've had the opportunity to learn. At the same time, it's important to acknowledge that the journey and the lessons didn't end on that day in the park, just as it didn't end when I spread my father's ashes in the ocean in Cape Town. In the years since, I have had my ups and downs. Life has taught me many new lessons as well as reminders of lessons I thought I knew.

I've had the good fortune of marrying my best friend, Sonya. I have gone to graduate school. I've also had the opportunity to launch a business Sonya and I co-founded called Nature Unplugged. And I've been through some challenging times, such as caretaking for my mom as she dealt with depression and anxiety several years ago. It was during that time of helping my mom that

I wrote the majority of this book. While it was difficult, it was also a time of great learning. It was an opportunity to put the lessons I had learned from my dad's life and death to work. The lessons helped ground and support me throughout.

One of my biggest takeaways has been the major difference between intellectually understanding a concept and putting it into practice. Once I had "completed" my quest to learn about my dad and his death, I thought my work was finished. Cognitively grasping the lessons was just the beginning. It didn't take too long to do that, but applying them to life, especially when things got tough, was another story.

The shift from cognitive understanding to a more embodied knowing has inspired me to view the lessons in a different light. When I first wrote the lessons, I framed them in a negative perspective. In other words, they were based on what *not* to do. While they served a purpose for a time, I'd now like to reframe what I wrote through a positive lens.

Lesson 1: ~~Racing Through Life~~ Slow Down

Take time to appreciate the present moment, which, of course, is the only moment we ever actually experience.

Lesson 2: ~~Focusing on Money, Image, and Status~~ Focus on Personal Growth, Relationships, and Helping Others

Focus on cultivating forms of intrinsic motivation like personal growth, relationships, and helping others. There is certainly a place for focusing on money, image, status, and other sources of extrinsic motivation. However, be mindful not to let those things define your sense of self-worth (as they did for my father).

Lesson 3: ~~All or Nothing~~ Both/And

Life isn't all or nothing, winning or losing, success or failure, black or white. There are many different shades and nuances. It's important to be able to take various perspectives. Instead of either/or, consider approaching things with the mindset of both/and.

Lesson 4: ~~Fighting with Reality~~ Make Friends with Reality

Reality is going to keep on doing its thing with or without you. Accepting what is beyond your control is empowering. I'm not saying to be complacent or to stay stuck in situations you don't like and can change. Go after what you want *and* practice acceptance. In the long run, it's much easier (and more peaceful) to make friends with what "is" rather than oppose it.

In the process of uncovering my dad's story and in helping my mom, I've explored and studied these lessons in depth. In my academic pursuits, I've had the opportunity to gather research that supports these lessons. Additionally, I've worked with some incredible doctors, psychiatrists, psychologists, and other medical and mental health-care professionals who have helped reinforce these lessons along the way.

When I first sat down to write this book, I envisioned there being a series of steps for how to move through dealing with this type of loss. Ideally in a replicable and streamlined manner. I wish I could tell you that there were four steps to overcoming the death of a loved one by suicide, but it's not that easy. While the lessons I learned from my dad's suicide are helpful pointers, I don't believe that there is a formula for how to deal with this sort of thing. Everyone is going to have their own unique circumstances and path. We all have the choice of how we interpret what happens in our lives. The key, I believe, is to develop a mindset of curiosity and to see that there is no shortage of opportunities to learn and raise our awareness.

While everyone will have their own path on this journey, it's important to remember we are not alone. Many of us have been affected, whether personally or through a friend or loved one, by mental illness and/or suicide. There is a part for all of us to play in working to raise awareness and to overcome the stigma around suicide and mental illness. My hope is that this book serves as an inspiration to others to share the stories that need to be shared and to listen deeply to the stories that need to be heard.

RESOURCES

For more information about Sebastian and his work, visit WWW.NATUREUNPLUGGED.COM. Nature Unplugged was co-founded by Sebastian and Sonya, his wife and partner, with the purpose of cultivating wellness through healthier relationships with technology and a deeper connection to nature. Nature Unplugged facilitates workshops and retreats and offers individual and group coaching.

NatureUnplugged.com has additional resources on topics such as mindfulness, meditation, and yoga. There are also tools and resources on how to help create healthier relationships with technology, and ways to encourage deeper connections with nature. To connect with Sebastian directly, email: sebastian@natureunplugged.com.

ACKNOWLEDGMENTS

I AM DEEPLY GRATEFUL FOR ALL THE PEOPLE WHO HAVE HELPED BRING THIS BOOK TO LIFE. To my wife, Sonya, for her companionship, patience, and love throughout this process. To the family, friends, teachers, and mentors who helped guide me along the way, some of whom I've mentioned here and many I haven't: the Kennedys, the Colvins, the Neumanns, the Bonneys, Derelynn and Michael Kalafer, the Spences, the Lees, the Thompsons, the Mahers, the Chartrands, Devon Hedding, Matt Lamkin, Ben Zoldan, Alice Bandy, Jaime Chambers, Dr. Mark Kalina, Dr. Gregory Dickson, Liz Mohamed, Michael Jackson, Pablo and Nancy Pollard. To Donn "Bernie" Bernstein, for your timeless friendship, inspiration, and creative guidance. To Patti Fox, for your ceaseless belief, love, and support along the way. To John Maher, for your friendship and inspiration over the years and for the amazing cover photo.

To my professors and mentors at the University of San Diego: Liz Mueller, Dr. Lorri Sulpizio, Dr. Ana Estrada, Dr. Michael Lindsay, Dr. Conor Mclaughlin, Dr. Zachary Green, and Dr. Stefano Olmeti. Thank you for your dedication, encouragement, and guidance. To my advisor and mentor Dr. Terri Monroe, thank you for the work you do.

To my amazing editor and publishing partner, Bethany Kelly, thank you for your clarity and support. To Frank Steele, for your editing, insights, and help in refining this book. To Stefan Merour, thank you for your vision in the design. To Totran Mai,

.e beautiful map. To Kellie Shay Hinze, Jon Hinze, Kristin ᴗuthbertson, Ian Chartrand, and Julie Jakopic for their insights and help with the manuscript during its early stages.

I would like to express my gratitude for two dear friends and mentors who passed away before this book was published, Richard Farson and Reed Thompson. Richard, thank you for listening and for sharing your incredible wisdom. Although I didn't write of our conversations in this book, you played a monumental role in guiding my path. To Reed, thank you for everything. I couldn't have asked for a better role model.

To my mom, Susan, and sister, Tanasa, for all your love and support along this wild ride. Your courage and strength is an inspiration to me. I couldn't have done this without you. Finally, I wish to honor my dad, Vernon, for being the greatest teacher I could have ever asked for.

ABOUT THE AUTHOR

SINCE HE CAN REMEMBER, NATURE HAS BEEN A CENTRAL PART OF SEBASTIAN'S LIFE. He was fortunate to grow up in the beach community of La Jolla, California, and spent his childhood mixing it up in the ocean. As a young boy, he lost his father to suicide, which would later deeply inspire his path in life. As a young adult, he had the opportunity to travel extensively and experience many of the world's great surf spots as a professional bodyboarder. Through his travel, Sebastian developed a deep love and appreciation for our natural world, and at the same time was drawn to the practice of yoga.

His love for yoga led him to study at Prana Yoga Center in La Jolla, California, and his passion for nature eventually led him to pursue a BA in Environment and Natural Resource Conservation at San Diego State University. He also holds an MA in Leadership Studies from the University of San Diego.

He lives with his wife Sonya in Encinitas, California. He and Sonya have a business called Nature Unplugged, which focuses on cultivating wellness through healthier relationships with technology and a deeper connection to nature. When he is not writing or working on Nature Unplugged, Sebastian enjoys swimming, bodysurfing, surfing, and stand-up paddling (pretty much all things) in the wild Pacific Ocean.